Con

I. Systematic Field Investigation of a Kill Site

Purpose

THIS FIELD MANUAL is designed to help anyone determine whether an animal was killed by a large predator and which species was involved with the predation event.

It intends to improve the accuracy of identifying the predator responsible for killing an animal.

It intends to improve consistency among those using this manual when investigating predation events.

It intends to clarify and define the terminology used in classifying a predation event.

Ultimately, this manual intends to improve our understanding of predator-prey relationships, to inform science-based wildlife management decisions.

Acknowledgments

SAFARI CLUB INTERNATIONAL Foundation (SCIF) and the SCIF Hunter Legacy Fund sponsored the production and publication of this manual, demonstrating one of the many contributions hunter-supported conservation organizations have made to wildlife research and management.

Dr. Jerry Belant, Dr. Harold Picton, Jim Hammill, Dr. Bob Inman, and Dr. Jon Swenson provided key insight and review of portions of this manual. We thank Dr. James Halfpenny for key final content edits and graciously allowing the inclusion of thirteen pages from his 1986 publication, *A Field Guide to Mammal Tracking in North America.*

We thank those field professionals who from their years of experience, unselfishly and collectively contributed the content for this manual, providing a useful tool for those in the field conducting wildlife management and research. The basic knowledge and insight found in this manual was contributed from the following wildlife professionals:

- Matthew Lewis, Director of Conservation, Safari Club
- Bryan Aber, Carnivore Biologist, ID Fish and Game
- Liz Bradley, Species Management Specialist, MT Fish, Wildlife & Parks (MTFWP)
- Mark Bruscino, Large Carnivore Program Supervisor, WY Game and Fish

- Peggy Callahan, Executive Director, Wildlife Science Center, MN
- Kevin Frey, Species Management Specialist, MTFWP
- Steve Gullage, Senior Programs Manager, Conservation Visions Inc.
- Dr. Al Harmata, Affiliate Faculty, Montana State University
- Ben Jimenez, Bitterroot Elk Ecology Project, MTFWP
- Jamie Jonkel, Species Management Specialist, MTFWP
- Nathan Lance, Species Management Specialist, MTFWP
- Larry Lewis, Wildlife Technician & Fish and Game Peace Officer, AK Fish and Game
- Shane Mahoney, President and CEO, Conservation Visions Inc.
- Tim Manley, Species Management Specialist, MTFWP
- Dr. Kerry Murphy, District Biologist, Bridger Teton NF, US Forest Service
- Abigail Nelson, Species Management Specialist, MTFWP
- Dr. Jennifer Ramsey, DVM, Wildlife Veterinarian, MTFWP
- Dr. Tom Roffe, DVM PhD, Chief of Wildlife Health, US Fish and Wildlife Service
- Mike Ross, Species Management Specialist, MTFWP
- Dr. Toni Ruth, Research Scientist, Selway Institute
- Dr. Doug Smith, Wolf Research Project Leader, Yellowstone National Park, US National Park Service
- Dr. Frank van Manen, Supervisory Research Wildlife Biologist, Team Leader Interagency Grizzly Bear Study Team, US Geological Survey
- Jennifer Vashon, Wildlife Biologist, Species Specialist for lynx and black bear, Maine Department of Inland Fisheries and Wildlife

Preface

"Understanding the relationships between predators and prey is essential for wildlife managers
to make science-based decisions with managing
wildlife."

—Shane Mahoney, personal communication

OUR UNDERSTANDING OF predator-prey dynam-
ics is often limited by our inability to accurately identify
what species of predator is responsible for killing prey. This
understanding is crucial when developing management
strategies for both predator and prey populations. It is also
important for effective management of livestock depredation.
While this manual may have multiple applications, it strives
to distinguish the signs left by different large predators when
killing and consuming wild prey.

It is unreasonable to expect even the most experienced
biologists to solve every wildlife predation mystery at the scene
of a kill. When an investigation of a kill site fails to solve the
mystery, the upshot is commonly noted as "Unknown Predator." The higher the percentage of kill sites in the same study
or ecosystem noted as "Unknown Predator," the lower our

confidence becomes when concluding what predator species is dominant. Knowing to what extent a predator is dominant is central for estimating its holistic impact on a prey population. Our science-based approach in managing wildlife in predator-rich systems drastically improves when we understand the role of each predator. Thus, the more mysteries we can solve, the better, and the more guidance we have to solve the mysteries, the better. This manual consolidates the expertise of twenty wildlife professionals with over 420 years of collective field experience and offers it to the next generation of biologists to build on.

Introduction

FIELD BIOLOGISTS INVESTIGATE kill sites of animals to better understand the interactions between predators and prey. Mentally recreating the predation event from the stalking predator at a vantage point, the chase, the kill, and how the protein reward is consumed is exhilarating. Biologists live vicariously through this raw reality of nature and have their own glimpse at what it means to be wild.

While exciting, recreating a predation event only from sparse clues left behind is difficult and can be frustrating. Investigators spend hours second-guessing themselves while exhausting every possibility from inconclusive evidence. Nonetheless, the purpose is important, and in the end, each biologist is working towards a goal of improving the science in wildlife management.

Wildlife managers must consider many factors affecting wildlife, including cause-specific mortality from disease, starvation, trauma, and predation. Insights into causes of mortality are time consuming and expensive to obtain, yet essential in developing successful wildlife management strategies. Fortunately, cumulative knowledge and technological advancements have dramatically improved our ability to determine how and why an animal died.

Traditionally, physical evidence found on and around a carcass was used to determine whether and how an animal was killed. Commonly used evidence included age and condition of prey, signs that the animal was killed and consumed, prey caching, habitat type, hair samples, footprints found at the site, and so on. Since the late 1990s, our understanding of predator behavior has been enhanced through increasingly sophisticated research techniques. DNA technology now allows us to determine species involved by obtaining saliva samples from puncture wounds. Innovations in technology from GPS, mortality sensors, vaginal implant transmitters, micro transmitters that can be placed on neonates, trail cameras, and so on have allowed wildlife professionals to more fully understand and accurately assess predation at kill sites. However, even with technological advancements, the basics of field investigation are as important today as they were thirty years ago. Technology cannot replace how the human brain can collect all the clues to recreate the events that transpired at a kill site. We invest in new technology because it provides tools and information to improve our ability to conduct consistent and accurate kill site investigations.

The confidence or likelihood in identifying the species involved in a predation event can range from definitive (actually observing the event) to unknown (no clear evidence of predation). Unless a predation event is observed, it can be difficult to determine what predator killed a prey, especially when evidence of more than one predator species is found scavenging the kill site. The classification of the event is based on evidence observed and collected during the field investigation, with potential follow-up laboratory tests. Under most circumstances, multiple lines of evidence are needed to identify the predator species involved and the level of certainty in the determination.

Several factors are working against the investigator of a kill site. A carcass is often scavenged by several species of predators before an investigator locates it. This scavenging can be rotational between different species. Scavenging can mask or confuse identification of the species responsible for actually killing the prey. For instance, a bear can consume a large portion of a carcass in a short amount of time and erase the evidence left by a coyote. Brown bears have been observed displacing wolves, and wolves have been seen displacing both brown and black bears off carcasses. Both wolves and brown bears have been known to seize cougar kills. Therefore it is important to investigate the remains and also search the kill site and vicinity for day beds, latrine sites, and signs of pursuit.

Time is also not on our side. In most situations it is critical to minimize the length of time between the death of an animal and necropsy. Evidence will literally disappear over time, and there can be a short window (hours to a few days) for determining predation. Weather events (snow, rain, large temperature changes) occurring between predation and investigation can mask evidence at the scene or wash it away. Decomposition and scavenging also degrade the carcass over time, erasing signs of predation. The amount of time that passes after a prey is killed will affect the degree of confidence in classifying the event.

Many times there are few clues and remains from which to glean evidence of predation. When only pieces of a carcass or a radio collar are found at a kill site, determining whether a predation even occurred may be impossible, especially if there was no sign of a struggle. If neonates are involved, there may be little to nothing left to ascertain an animal was even killed. Because neonates can be entirely consumed, it is critical to use technology (such as vaginal implant transmitters, neonate transmitters, and mortality sensors) to accurately evaluate predation impacts in studies attempting to evaluate birth, mortality and recruitment rates.

This manual will guide the user through a systematic process of gathering evidence to make an informed assessment as to whether cause of death was by predation, and if so, the predator species most likely involved. In addition, this manual provides a template defining the terminology in event classification (definitive, probable, possible, unknown, or other). Descriptions and pictures of signs left by predators on different carcasses including consumption and scavenging behaviors are offered as guidance. The focus of this manual is on large prey animals, mainly ungulates. Specific characteristics of eight widely distributed North American predator species (cougar, brown bear, black bear, wolf, coyote, lynx, bobcat, or wolverine) are documented according to strategies for killing and carcass consumption of large ungulates.

Determining predation is an inexact science. Predation can be certain if there are signs of pursuit and/or hemorrhaging, i.e., internal bleeding that only occurs if an animal is still alive. If direct evidence is not present, the event may be assigned to a species with a level of uncertainty described as probable or possible. With careful consideration of all the evidence found, it will likely be a "weight of evidence" consideration that is used to classify many predation events. This is both the challenge and the reward involved in discovery.

I. Systematic Field Investigation of a Kill Site

A COMMON MISTAKE when investigating a carcass is rushing to conclusions before all of the evidence has been evaluated. Unless the kill is witnessed, no single piece of information may be conclusive. Although predator species have distinctive killing and scavenging behaviors, many of those behaviors overlap between species. It is also common for predators to scavenge kills made by other predator species.

Use of multiple lines of evidence is critical when determining the species most likely responsible for the predation. The more evidence you have that points to a suspect species, the greater degree of certainty in the conclusion. Experience, attention to detail, and using a standardized approach is essential in making accurate and consistent conclusions. The following guideline provides a systematic process of evaluating a predation/scavenging event.

Get Organized

Before going into the field, ensure that all of your equipment is in excellent condition and well organized. Organization improves efficiency and consistency, and it ensures you aren't missing critical equipment. Durable tool bags and tackle boxes can be used to keep equipment organized.

Appendix A provides an example of a field collection kit and a list of equipment useful for field personnel. In addition, make sure you are prepared to properly document your observations, including taking lots of digital pictures.

Safety Considerations

Use extreme caution in approaching a carcass, not only for reasons of personal safety, but also to protect the integrity of the overall site and any direct evidence of cause of death. Although it is important to investigate as soon as possible, displacing some species is dangerous. Make noise, stay alert, and work with another person if bears are a part of the ecosystem. If the carcass is fresh and active feeding by bears or lions is apparent, leave and return two to four days later unless public safety or other considerations dictate immediate intervention. Carry bear spray and/or a firearm and be proficient in their use.

Wild animals carry diseases and parasites that can be contracted by humans. Therefore, proper safety precautions should be taken to prevent exposure when handling evidence and investigating a carcass. The post-mortem health status of the animal being investigated is unknown. Therefore, during carcass handling, tissue collection, and so on, the investigator should always wear nitrile or latex gloves, mask and eye protection to prevent/minimize exposure to pathogens such as parasites (*Echinococcus granulosus*) and bacteria (*Mycobacterium bovis, Brucella abortus*). A respiratory mask is highly recommended due to potential of exposure through airborne routes. Eye protection will help the investigator to avoid getting splashed in the eye by body fluids during necropsy of a carcass.

It is recommended that field personnel maintain good rapport with a wildlife veterinarian, if one is available. In addition, if you develop a sickness, immediately contact a physician. Describe to the physician the type of work you do and that you may have been exposed to pathogens they may not normally confront.

Investigation: There are five general phases that involve collecting, documenting, and cumulatively assessing evidence when determining cause of death by predation. The five phases are:

Phase 1: Initial overview of carcass site and its surrounding area.

Phase 2: Focus on carcass and immediate carcass site.

Phase 3: Investigate carcass for signs of hemorrhaging.

Phase 4: Summarize all evidence and their interrelationship.

Phase 5: Weight of evidence and event classification.

An example of a data sheet, guided by the five phases of predation investigation outlined in this manual, is provided in Appendix D. Investigators may choose to modify data sheets to their needs specific to active research projects using radio-telemetry, marked animals, and so on.

Throughout the investigation, it is important to continually ask, "Are there signs of predation?"

Phase 1. Initial Overview of Carcass Site and Surrounding Area

Do not go immediately to the carcass. Use your knowledge and previous experience to visualize what may have happened from a distance. Then imagine the carcass as the center of an archery target and investigate each outer ring, working toward the bull's-eye. Move slowly, noting or collecting evidence as you proceed. If helpful, flag evidence for later collection or further examination.

Characterize the habitat around the kill site. Is it open meadow, shrub/grassland, or forested? What is the overstory and understory cover? Also make note of general topography, aspect and terrain features such as rock outcroppings, proximity to roads, and proximity to human activity such as residential, agricultural, mining, or timber harvest. Is it habitat with high security conducive to ambush or is it more open habitat conducive to a chase? The juxtaposition of these characteristics in combination with understanding how and where each predator prefers to hunt may give you some indication to the species likely hunting there. It also may provide insight for evidence collection.

As your investigation proceeds toward the carcass, note any and all sign. Record fresh tracks, track size and stride by species. Track size, pattern, and stride (Appendix C, excerpts from *A Field Guide to Mammal Tracking in North America*, Halfpenny, 1986) can be useful in determining relative age of the predator (adult, sub-adult, juvenile) and also the type of attack (ambush versus pursuit) of the prey.

Scrutinize surrounding vegetation for recent trails through tall grass, drag trails, trampled vegetation, broken shrub/twigs, signs of a struggle, and blood. Try to determine the prey's path to where it died or was killed. A blue light can be helpful in finding blood sign.

In this initial phase, many biologists view an effective search area to be a 200-meter radius from the carcass. Search for beds, latrine sites, scrapes under trees, recently disturbed soil, and signs of a chase. Signs of a chase may include hair, blood, and broken twigs. As you proceed, identify and collect hair and scat. Also note presence and activity of scavenging birds.

When you get to the carcass, use your perspective of the entire scene to help determine if the cause of death was from natural causes. There will be times when the cause of death is obvious, such as when an animal falls off a rock ledge, drowns, succumbs to disease or infection, gets trapped in a deep hole, or suffers a debilitating injury, such as from a vehicle collision. Obvious causes of death will save time in arriving at a conclusion and lead more quickly to a full mortality assessment. However, we emphasize that although the cause of death may appear obvious, evaluating the entire kill site and larger landscape provides standardization and confidence in the investigator's conclusion.

Phase 2. Focus on Carcass and Immediate Carcass Site

The various circumstances under which an animal can die include: degenerative, anomalous, metabolic, nutritional, neoplastic, infectious and immune, trauma and toxic (Roffe and Work, 2005). Although we are focusing primarily on trauma, the above list is an important reminder that one should not jump to conclusions. After all, there are many ways that an animal can die.

a) Time of Death

Determining time of death is problematic. The good news is that an accurate time of death is not as important as getting to the carcass as soon as possible after death. Time of death can help you determine what predators killed the animal. For example, if an animal is killed at night, the predator is likely not avian.

Reaching the carcass quickly after death is critical in determining if a predator killed the animal. Fortunately, technology has shortened that time in predator-prey research. Radio-telemetry units that have mortality sensors, remotely downloadable Global Positioning Systems (GPS) technology, or Very High Frequency (VHF) with store-on-board GPS collars are commonly used to quickly identify mortality. Be aware that capture myopathy may be a cause of death when handling animals. Death within a few hours or even days after capture would lead to suspicion of a capture myopathy effect (Dr. Tom Roffe, personal communication).

If the carcass is not reached soon after death, the various stages of decomposition and scavenging may complicate the investigation. Decomposition is a function of animal size, mass, and ambient conditions. Payne (1965) described six stages of decomposition: fresh, bloat, active decay, advanced decay, dry, and remains. Factors that affect decomposition and therefore time of death estimates include season, weather changes, temperature, insect abundance, scavenging, habitat type, and so on. (Stroud unknown date, Dillon 1997, Gonder 2008).

In some instances carcass decomposition can be delayed due to environmental influences. For example, animals that die during winter months can remain frozen until spring, delaying decomposition. Such a carcass will appear to have died more recently based solely on decomposition.

Recent advancements in wildlife forensics involve evaluating insect colonization, metamorphosis and species succession throughout the decomposition process, as well as other factors, including patterns of tooth cracking, changes in odor, and so on (Gonder, 2008). Most of this work is directed toward time of death determination in cases applied to wildlife enforcement.

Scavenging can literally eliminate evidence as related to the six stages. A carcass can be reduced to hair and bones after five days (or less) by scavenging. Even when tissues are left on the carcass, the stage of decomposition can be accelerated because of scavenging. Based on size of the prey, or in the case of wolves and sometimes coyotes, the number of individuals in a pack, the prey may be consumed even before scavenging can occur.

Scavenging can resemble predation when an animal may have died of natural causes. Without direct signs of predation (hemorrhaging, pursuit, direct observation), the investigator will be left estimating a likelihood of predation.

b) Condition at Time of Death

It is important to understand that both immediate and gradual causes of death may be at play. An animal in poor condition or health may be near death and may have died had it not been killed by a predator. On the other hand, a healthy animal may have become weakened or encumbered (e.g. blindness, deafness), making it more vulnerable to predation. Therefore, examining body condition of the killed prey can tell us many things about predator-prey relationships, such as strengthening or weakening assumptions of prey vulnerability/availability to predation.

Several factors are useful for evaluating the condition of an animal at the time of death. Look for other signs of prior trauma-induced injury such as previously broken bones that have healed, older soft tissue damage, hemorrhaging without tooth or claw marks on inside of skin, or obvious signs of infection or disease. Bone marrow fat and fat tissues that surround muscles and organs can be indicators of condition. Marrow bones are often left behind while organs such as the kidneys and body fat can be entirely consumed by the time you find the kill site.

There are two types of bone marrow. Red marrow basically produces red and white blood cells and platelets. Red marrow is found in flat bones, such as the pelvis, and also in the ends of the long bones, such as the femur, tibia, humerus, and ulna. Yellow marrow is mainly comprised of fat, and when an animal is malnourished or is not producing enough blood, the body uses the marrow fat as a last resort for energy and converts yellow marrow to red marrow to assist with blood cell production. When assessing body condition, you should look at the yellow marrow, which is located in the center hollow space of the long bones. Healthy bone marrow fat can be visually classified as white, solid, and waxy. Malnourished bone marrow fat looks red, yet solid. Poor bone marrow fat condition appears red and gelatinous (Cheatum 1949). With some experience it will become easy to distinguish these differences.

**Femur Bone Marrow
Good Quality**

Femur bone marrow, good quality.

Femur bone marrow, poor quality.

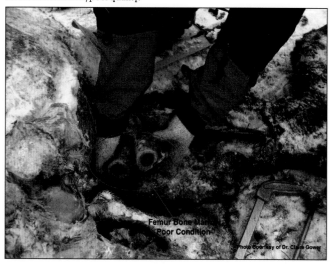

Femur Bone Marrow
Poor Condition

Marrow fat content can also be measured in femur bones using a compression method as described by Greer (1968). Femur marrow fat content in elk has been correlated with both metatarsus and mandibular marrow (Husseman et. al. 2003). Collecting a mandible may be useful in circumstances of predation when a femur is not available. Mech (1985) agreed that marrow fat can indicate poor condition, but cautioned that healthy marrow does not necessarily indicate a healthy animal in good condition.

The lower jaw can also be used to determine the animal's age by using the tooth wear and replacement method (Quimby and Gaab 1957). However, teeth wear differently in different habitats with different forage bases. If the animal already has its permanent dentition, it is best to reference "wear guidelines" or "jaw boards" of known ages from the geographical area of collection. A more exact age can be determined from cementum age analysis or pulp cavity density. For cementum age, extract a middle incisor (I_1) for analysis. For pulp cavity density, extract the first premolar (P_2) for X-ray analysis.

c) Natural Death and Minimal Scavenging

Consider all explanations of how an animal died. Just because an animal is dead does not mean it was killed. Document the clear absence of predation and any gross evidence associated from other causes of mortality. For example, sick or injured animals tend to move into thick cover or downhill toward a water source. Look for tracks or other physical evidence that could indicate such movements. Other indicators of non-predation-related deaths include: legs are folded into or under the body as if it has bedded, carcass has remained stationary leaving a body imprint on the ground, evidence of repeated weak attempts to get up indicated by leg or head scraping or scratching in soil or snow, and legs and skeleton remaining generally connected via various remaining tissues. There should be no evidence of pursuit, struggle, or predator-caused trauma, such as hemorrhaging.

Depending on wildlife disease concerns in the geographic area, field personnel should understand that these carcasses might be important to your local wildlife veterinarian regarding disease surveillance efforts. The equipment listed in Appendix A would enable the investigator to collect relevant tissues for lab analysis.

d) Ruling Out Other Predators

<u>Avian</u>: Eagle predation can add complexity in determining predation. The investigator should be aware of raptor kill characteristics. The following description is based on personal communication with James Halfpenny. Front talon punctures can be one to three inches and the hallux to a front talon can be four to six inches apart, respectively. The puncture wounds are deeper than teeth, triangular, and long. Compression fractures of the skull and multiple wounds to upper back and ribs may be evident. Puncture wounds can be found on internal organs. The skin on the prey may be inside out, with the inside of the skin cleaned. Major hemorrhages are often not found, possibly due to ingestion of tissue at sites of hemorrhaging and/or wounding. Again, if there is no indication of hemorrhaging, and characteristics above are evident, it is likely scavenging not predation (Dr. Al Harmata, personal communication). In addition,

muscle tissue can appear to be picked clean off the bones of small prey, such as neonates, and in the absence of scavenging, there would be no sign of chewing on the bones.

<u>Domestic Dogs</u>: Predation by domestic dogs can also confuse predation determination. The following description is based on personal communication with James Halfpenny. Domestic dog predation behavior is more often a result of predator chase response, rather than predation followed by carcass consumption. The attack and wounding can be described as sloppy, unmethodical, and ineffective. Prey are often not immediately killed, with injuries often resulting in death within two to three days. The carcass may be found near or far from the attack site. The carcass will likely have multiple wound sites; the udder is often torn and ripped. The throat seldom shows signs of attack. Therefore, be cognizant of domestic dog presence in the area of a kill site, such as near homes or popular dog walking areas. Dogs are often present in seemingly remote areas, where they may even be feral and prey on wildlife as a food source.

e) Human-Caused Death

A carcass found near a road may have died from a vehicle collision. Although vehicle collisions usually result in severe injuries, the animal may have moved some distance from the road prior to death. Look for evidence of extensive hemorrhaging, broken bones, and abraded skin suggesting vehicle and road impact.

The possibility of a human-caused wound, especially during and shortly after hunting seasons, should be considered and investigated for bullet or arrow entry and exit wounds. Also look for hair pushed into the carcass or through the hide from a bullet or arrow, straight cuts in the hide and on bones left by a knife, small diameter holes in hide or bones from less obvious shot fired by a shotgun, or whether antlers or horns are missing from the site.

f) Hair and Scat Collection and Track Identification

Finding physical evidence of a predator may not be easy. Locations likely to contain hairs of a predator include caches, day beds, bark on trees near caches or beds, shrubs, fences, and the area of pursuit and struggle. Blowing air into a day bed causes hair to twirl around and makes it easier to see and collect. It is best to collect guard hairs, but underfur can also aid in identification. Although several hair identification guides are available (such as Moore et. al. 1995), we suggest you make or use a region-specific hair reference guide.

Scat may have species-specific characteristics in size, shape, and texture. Photograph and measure scat samples prior to its collection, before your handling alters the shape or appearance. A field guide can be used to identify the species at a later date.

Discovering tracks of a predator will vary in difficulty depending on the substrate and wetness of the ground surface. Identify predator tracks, including size and stride to the best of your ability (Halfpenny 2008, 2010, and Appendix C, excerpts from *A Field Guide to Mammal Tacking in North America*, Halfpenny, 1986). A guide specifically developed for track identification should also be carried and used on site.

g) Summary of General Qualitative Characteristics of Ungulate Kill Sites and Gross Examination of Carcasses Categorized by Felid, Ursid, and Canid Predators

The following table is meant to help the investigator make a general classification to family of predators based on attack and feeding behavior, understanding that many of the behaviors will overlap slightly or extensively.

TABLE 1

EVIDENCE	FELID	URSID	CANID
Kill site	tidy	somewhat tidy	messy
Carcass moved or dragged to shelter or cached	yes	yes	no (coyotes may cache or hide smaller prey)
Cache w/light surface debris/ hair	yes	no	no (coyotes may cache or hide smaller prey)
Cache w/excavation and large debris	no	yes	no
"Banana peel" effect on hide	no	yes	no
Plucked hair	yes	no	no
Inside of hide licked clean (J. Halfpenny personal communication)	yes	occasionally	no
Rumen/intestine	not consumed	consumed, strewn around	sometimes portions consumed

(continued)

TABLE 1 (CONTINUED)

EVIDENCE	FELID	URSID	CANID
Attack points	neck, throat, shoulders	head, dorsal midline (spine), crushed vertebrae, broken pelvis	many different attack points, legs, hindquarters, flank, "armpits," lower shoulders, and nose
Claw marks	yes	yes	no
Initial feeding pattern	through rib cage, behind shoulder or lower abdomen just anterior to pelvic juncture	usually abdomen, but can occur through rib cage or other areas	abdomen, hindquarters, at times everywhere depending on number of individuals present
Sign of pursuit	no or short	variable	yes
Bed sites	up to 200 meters from cache, at base of tree/rocks	very near or on top of the cache	many bed sites and feeding sites in vicinity of carcass
Latrine	yes	no	no
Remains	in defined area (unless scavenged by canids)	in defined area (unless scavenged by canids)	strewn all over

Note: No one piece of evidence is absolute. The investigator needs to evaluate all available evidence.

Phase 3. Investigate Carcass for Hemorrhaging

h) Hemorrhaging

Hemorrhaging results from injury and can only occur when the animal is alive. Subcutaneous hemorrhaging occurs inside the body when an injury occurs, resulting in internal bleeding.

"The inside of the hide is a blueprint of what happened on the outside." (Mark Brucino personal communication, 2012) When an animal is attacked, there will be hemorrhaging in the muscle tissue; blood, resulting from bleeding from the muscle, is usually found between the wounded muscle and the skin (subcutaneous). Carefully skin back the hide and look for hemorrhaging from ante-mortem (pre-death) wounds. Look also for signs of aspirated blood in the nose, mouth, and/or trachea, indicating an injury that allowed blood to enter the respiratory system during a prolonged pursuit or struggle. Look for evidence of a bullet or arrow wound and associated hemorrhaging.

Even if most of the muscle tissue has been consumed, you will likely find puncture holes in the hide if a predator killed the animal. Take special care when inspecting the hide on the neck. Carefully cut through puncture holes and determine whether the area around the puncture is swollen. Swelling of tissues around the puncture indicates hemorrhaging and the area may be discolored. Once skinned, you can hold the hide toward the sun, looking from the inside out, to more readily observe claw marks, teeth scrapes, and punctures. Road-killed ungulates often have severe hemorrhaging, but not hemorrhaging associated with the puncture injuries described above. Prey that died from natural causes and were scavenged would not have hemorrhaging associated with puncture injuries.

All postmortem wounds will not show signs of hemorrhaging. However, if you are looking at wounds on the side of the carcass lying on the ground, you may see a pooling of blood between the skin and muscle tissue. This pooling effect is actually the result of body fluids draining to the low point of the carcass (lavitity). The tissues on top are pale and puncture wounds have no signs of swelling. Lavitity can look like hemorrhaging.

Location(s) of hemorrhaging is an important diagnostic because different predators have different attack strategies. Hemorrhaging in the hindquarters, legs, and lower shoulders together would indicate a canid, even though there are obvious signs of bear feeding behavior. By contrast, if there are obvious signs of hemorrhaging on the head and dorsal areas of shoulders and neck, but it appears that wolves have been feeding heavily on the carcass, it is likely a bear kill.

If the animal is deer or calf size and there is not much sign of a struggle, hemorrhaging at the back of the skull and neck may indicate felid or avian. On larger prey, bite marks and hemorrhaging found on the throat and nose, along with claw marks and hemorrhaging on front shoulders, may also indicate felid.

i) Canine Measurements

Use caution in relying on canine separation measurements, which is the distance between the centers of canine puncture holes. A hide will stretch when it is fresh and shrink as it dries, so it can be difficult to obtain accurate measurements.

Multiple bites in the same area can occur, which confuses measurements. Importantly, there can be significant overlap between species such as bears, cougars, and wolves. As a reference, Dr. Toni Ruth (in prep 2013, Appendix B) uses the following measurements of canine punctures:

Cougar: 4.5 to 5.7 cm apart for upper canines; 3.0 to 4.5 cm apart for lower canines.

Wolf: 4.5 to 5.3 cm apart for upper canines; 3.0 to 4.0 apart for lower canines.

Brown Bear: 5.5 to 6.5 apart for upper canines; 5.5 to 6.5 apart for lower canines.

Black Bear: 4.5 to 5.5 apart for lower canines (canine measurements may overlap between an adult male black bear and an adult female brown bear).

Coyote: Bergman (et. al. 2010) reported 2.98 for upper canines (tip to tip) and 2.75 for lower canines (tip to tip).

Phase 4. General Hierarchy of Scavengers and Predatory Behavior

It is important to develop an understanding of the general order of dominance in scavenging of all predators in your geographic area of work.

As a general guideline, the order of species dominance in displacing other species scavenging at a kill site is as follows: brown bear, wolf, black bear, cougar, coyote, and lynx/bobcat. The wolverine is not considered a major predator in North American systems, and too little data is available to categorize its dominance in scavenging relative to other species.

Conversely, when evaluating a kill site with evidence of more than one predator species, consider which of the species present is most predatory in its behavior. For large-bodied prey, a general ranking of highest predatory behavior in descending order is cougar, wolf, brown bear, coyote, black bear.

With larger prey in systems with multiple large predators, additional considerations based on the above are:

i. Cougars are less likely to scavenge prey killed by other species. Cougars rarely displace other predators from a kill. They are more likely to make a kill and then be displaced from the carcass by other species, such as wolves or bears. Therefore, if cougars are part of the system, it is important to spend time looking for beds, latrines, tracks, and hair. You may have to look 200 meters from the carcass to find beds or latrines, which are likely to be found in a secure area (hiding cover such as cliff/rocks/ foliage) but with a view of the carcass/cache.

ii. Wolves kill ungulates throughout the year, while bears and coyotes are more likely to kill prey in spring/early summer and wounded animals in the fall, and scavenge outside of the calving/fawning periods. In addition, if bears have displaced wolves shortly after a wolf kill, the site will not have the messy, bone-and-tissue-scattered-everywhere appearance of a wolf kill.

iii. Bobcats, lynx, and wolverines are known to take deer, but typically kill much smaller prey than bears, wolves, coyotes, and cougars. Wolverines more often scavenge, than kill, larger prey. During spring and summer, all the predators described in this manual kill neonate ungulates, but there is little opportunity for competitive scavenging due to the small size of neonates. There is often little to no evidence left from neonate predation.

Phase 5. Summarizing All Evidence, Determining Weight of Evidence, and Event Classification

Unless the cause of death is obvious, there will come a point where you will summarize all the evidence collected and classify the event. What is the majority of evidence telling you? How confident are you in your conclusion? This manual uses categories for assessing certainty of the observer. The categories are: definitive; probable; possible; unknown; and not killed by predator. Figure 1 is a diagnostic key that provides a standardized and systematic approach to assigning likelihood to an event using these five categories. Unless there is direct evidence of predation, such as hemorrhaging, sign of pursuit or struggle, or direct observation of predation, an event is assigned a likelihood of predation.

Figure 1. Key to the Likelihood of a Predation Event

1. Evidence of predation (go to 2).
1. No evidence of predation (go to 4).

2. Direct evidence of predation—hemorrhaging, sign of pursuit or struggle, aspirated blood (nose, mouth, trachea). **DEFINITIVE.**

2. Indirect evidence of predation—kill site and carcass characteristics (go to 3).

3. Multiple lines of evidence including: moving carcass, caching, carcass hidden in cover, bed sites, fresh tracks and scat, skinning "banana peel" hide, rumen present or cached, skeletal bites, or only one predator present. **PROBABLE.**

3. Evidence through scavenging dominance (cougar displaced by other species, or only one predator present). **POSSIBLE.**

4. Evidence of scavenging (no direct or indirect evidence of predation), all sign old. **UNKNOWN.**

4. Little to no scavenging, signs of death other than predation. **NOT PREDATION.**

Dr. Toni Ruth has developed a matrix for the northern Rockies region that attempts to provide a systematic approach to event classification (Appendix B: Ruth in prep 2013). As this matrix is relevant for the northern Rockies region, it is strongly suggested that individuals develop an area-specific matrix for their own geographic region.

To date there has been no published standardized diagnostic key to classify the likelihood of a predation event by predator species. Figure 2 provides a dichotomous key, and uses the likelihood categories from the above key to help the investigator classify an event by predator species. This key may not represent all circumstances found in the field but will provide guidance in systematically characterizing an event relative to the five large predator species included in this manual.

Figure 2. Key to Classifying a Predation Event Using Kill, Kill Site, and Scavenging Characteristics for Cougar, Brown Bear, Black Bear, Wolf, and Coyote

1. Evidence of predation (go to 2).
1. No evidence of predation (go to 14).

2. Direct evidence of predation—Hemorrhaging (go to 3).
2. Indirect evidence of predation—kill site and carcass characteristics (go to 7).

3. Hemorrhaging on the front quarter to half of the carcass, no obvious pursuit, no aspirated blood (go to 4).
3. Hemorrhaging on legs, flanks, armpits, lower shoulders, lower hindquarters, face, and throat (can be massive from rear to front of carcass), obvious signs of pursuit, aspirated blood. **Definitive: Canid** (go to 6).

4. Hemorrhaging on face, throat, front of shoulders, back of neck with canine puncture wounds in those areas. Claw marks on face, shoulders, neck, back. Signs of carcass moved to cover/cache. Feeding into thoracic cavity through ribcage behind shoulder. Canine punctures (4.5-5.7 cm and 3.0-4.5 cm between upper and lower canines, respectively). **Definitive–Cougar.**
4. Hemorrhaging along dorsal midline, possibly on hindquarters/ribs and skull, crushed skull/cervical, thoracic (lumbar) vertebrae. Signs of carcass moved to cover/cache. May find claw marks at attack points. **Definitive: Ursid** (go to 5).

5. Use hair identification, Palmisciano Method for tracks (Appendix C) and canine measurements (5.5-6.5 cm and 5.5-6.5 cm between upper and lower canines, respectively). **Definitive: Brown Bear.**

5. Use hair identification, Palmisciano Method for tracks (Appendix C) and canine measurements (4.5-5.5 cm between lower canines). **Definitive: Black Bear.**

6. Use track measurements, canine measurements (4.5-5.3 cm and 3.0-4.5 cm between upper and lower canines, respectively), size of prey, and higher attack points on legs and body of prey to aid in distinguishing. **Definitive: Wolf.**

6. Use track measurements, canine measurements (2.98 cm and 2.75 tip to tip distances between upper and lower canines, respectively), and size of prey and lower attack points on legs and body of prey to aid in distinguishing. **Definitive: Coyote.**

7. Kill site characteristics (go to 8).

7. Evidence through (scavenging dominance and) scavenging (go to 12).

8. Tidy kill site, carcass moved/dragged to cover/cache (go to 9).

8. Messy kill site, no evidence of carcass being moved to cover or cached (go to 11).

9. Cached with light surface debris, plus hair. Plucked hair, rumen/intestine not consumed, latrine with fresh scat, bed with cougar hair, scrape, remains in defined area, fresh tracks. **Probable: Cougar.**

9. Cached with excavation and rough material—dirt, large sticks, rocks. Banana peel hide, bed site very near or right next to cache, remains in defined area, fresh tracks, scat, rumen/intestines consumed/strewn about. **Probable: Ursid** (go to 10).

10. Palmisciano Method track identification (Appendix C, Bear Family), scat, hair identification. **Probable: Brown Bear.**

10. Palmisciano Method track identification (Appendix C, Bear Family), scat, hair identification. **Probable: Black Bear.**

11. Large carcass strewn about the kill site at distances of 200 to 300 meters. Heavily disarticulated. May be many bed sites in spoke-like fashion around kill site (beds in open, on nearby ridges not oriented toward base of trees), hair and fresh tracks/scat and big bones heavily gnawed, ribs chewed down to vertebrae. **Probable: Wolf.**

11. Small carcass strewn about the kill site, less disarticulated than above, maybe a bed site, hair, fresh tracks/scat, and skeleton gnawing. **Probable: Coyote.**

12. Evidence of scavenging dominance (go to 13).

12. No evidence of scavenging dominance (go to 14).

13. Evidence of multiple predator presence, but has fresh cougar bed(s), latrine with fresh scat, fresh tracks, but no distinguishing characteristics of kill site or remains to distinguish predator. **Possible: Cougar.**

13. Evidence of only one predator present, and sign (scat, tracks) if present are older, weathered. **Possible: Species (sp) Present.**

14. Evidence of scavenging, all sign old, no diagnostic evidence of dominance, no direct or indirect evidence of predation. **Unknown.**

14. Little to no scavenging, signs of death other than predation. **Other.**

II. Characteristics of Kill and Kill Site by Species

Cougar (*Puma concolor*)

Cougars may often be the species that killed an animal, but bears, wolves, and coyotes will commonly scavenge the carcass, masking signs that would indicate that a cougar made the kill. Although the cougar is a stalking predator and more likely to kill in association with cover (such as along habitat edges), they occasionally scavenge vehicle kills, natural deaths, parts from hunter kills, and other lion kills, but generally not kills of more dominant carnivores. Cougars can stalk and kill in open areas. If the animal is large, it may be lightly cached there.

Attack points are focused on the front quarter of the animal. Attack points may be on the back of the neck, head (face), throat, and/or front shoulders. On smaller prey (such as deer, elk calves, bighorn sheep), killing bites will focus on the head (back of the head or skull, snapping vertebrae) or on the throat. On larger prey (such as adult elk) most of the killing bites are on the throat and/or nose, resulting in suffocation. Claw marks may be found on the head or shoulders, causing hemorrhaging in the muscle tissue in these locations. Felids have dewclaws, which can occasionally leave a fifth claw mark on prey (James Halfpenny, personal communication).

Cougars will usually enter the thoracic cavity (sometimes the upper abdomen) through the shoulder and rib cage, just behind the shoulder or in the lower abdomen anterior to the pelvic juncture. The entrance is clean and almost looks knife-like. They are likely to consume the organs in the upper body cavity first. Felids have a raspy tongue and can lick the inside of skin clean (James Halfpenny, personal communication).

Cougars will nearly always cache prey they have killed. Consumption can occur over several days on smaller prey and between six to ten days on larger prey. It is not unusual to have feeding followed by re-caching (several times) of larger prey. The carcass is moved to and cached in or near cover and

Intestines/stomach in tact

Ribcage

Photo Courtesy of Tim Thier

Cougar kill showing entry posterior of rib cage, NW Montana.

the actual behavior involves dragging surface debris, usually leaves, surface duff, snow, sand, and the like, combined with a noticeable amount of plucked hair. The cougar will usually bed within sight of the cache, again utilizing cover such as the base of a tree or rocks. With larger prey, such as adult elk, the carcass will likely be left where it died.

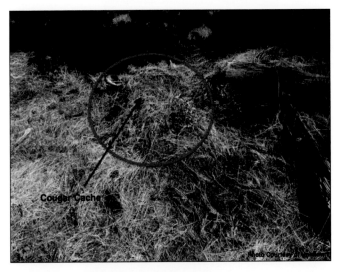

Cougar deer cache with light surface debris, Montana.

Cougar deer cache with heavier surface debris, Rocky Mountain Front, Montana.

IF YOU PACK IT IN! ...
PLEASE PACK IT OUT

Cougar Winter Cache

Photo Courtesy of Jim Williams

Attempt by cougar to cache Rocky Mountain bighorn sheep in winter, Rocky Mountain Front, Montana.

Cougars will usually have latrine sites. Most are nearer the bed site than the cache and are often covered with a mound of surface debris consisting of needles, leaf litter, or snow (resembling the arc and size of a garbage can lid, Toni Ruth personal communication). Upon investigation, it is not unusual to discover a number of scats in the latrine. Scrapes are sometimes found near kill sites.

Cougar scrape, Rocky Mountain Front, Montana.

Peculiar to cougars is a behavior called "plucking." Cougar will sheer "bunches" of hair from the carcass where they enter for feeding. Bunches of hair can be found on and near the feeding site and in cache debris.

Cougars in most cases will not consume the rumen or intestines. The rumen is often cached and/or found near the kill site, unless the carcass has been scavenged. It is not unlikely to find a carcass in the wintertime with the rumen contents frozen in a ball and untouched, if scavenging has not occurred.

Tracks, in combination with some of the characteristics above, are a strong indication that a cougar was the predator.

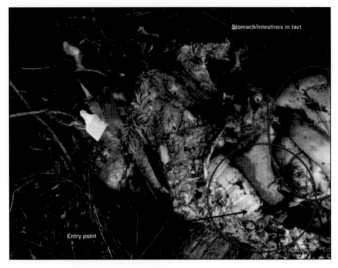

Cougar kill showing intestines and stomach intact and ribcage, NW Montana.

Brown (Grizzly) Bears (*Ursus arctos*)

Bears are better scavengers than predators. Brown bears are often a quick-attack predator; struggle is confined to a small area in space and time and, like cougars, found in association with habitat edge. However, brown bears have been known to pursue prey for several kilometers. Bears generally grab and eat newborn calves/fawns quickly, maybe leaving part of a leg, hoof, or hide. They have also been known to disable smaller prey with a side swat to the back/hips/pelvis.

Attack points on larger prey are generally focused dorsally in the head to shoulder area and right behind the shoulder blades, including the cervical and thoracic (sometimes lumbar) vertebrae. Blunt force trauma is diagnostic of a bear

Brown bear kill illustrating extensive hemorrhaging on shoulder, SW Montana.

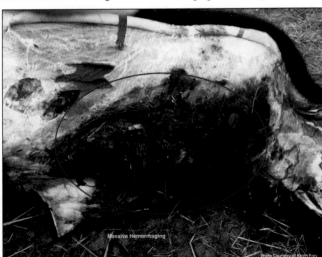

Brown bear kill, moose calf, Alaska.

A female moose and calf.

kill, with crushing of skull and vertebrae. Claw marks may be obvious. There will be significant hemorrhaging on the head and cervical and thoracic areas along the dorsal midline.

Bears often enter the carcass below the ribcage through the abdomen, eating most of the organ tissue and the rumen. The intestines are often strewn about the kill site. They will destroy many of the big bones, like femurs. An adult elk can be consumed by bears and other scavengers in two to five days.

Brown bears will likely cache a carcass, but not as reliably as a cougar. The carcass is usually moved and often cached near the kill site. The caching activity involves some excavation of dirt (a shallow bowl) and the carcass is covered with dirt, large sticks, and rocks. One contributor said, "It can look like really dirty meat." Bears tend to bed nearby, at times even on the cache itself.

Typical carcass appearance after being fed on by brown bear, SW Montana.

Brown bear cache

Photo Courtesy of Kevin Frey

Brown bear cache of elk showing debris, rocks, dirt, and so on, SW Montana.

Brown bear cache of moose, showing lighter debris, Alaska.

Cache

Brown bear cache of moose, Alaska.

Bears will peel the hide back, like a "banana peel," but usually don't eat much of the hide when consuming the carcass. What you see is a hide inverted back toward the foot with the lower leg bone sheared off. The hide has a skinned-out appearance.

Tracks are important for identifying the presence of bears. In geographical regions where black and brown bears overlap, it is important use track characteristics and hair identification to distinguish between the two species. **The Palmisciano Method is a distinguishing method when using a track from the front foot (Appendix C, Bear Family).** In addition, scat size can add information, but caution should be used due to similarities between species. Although the size/age of a bear are important, moisture content and fiber are critical factors affecting scat size (James Halfpenny personal communication)

Remains of elk calf killed and fed upon by a brown bear. Note skinned-out appearance, SW Montana.

Big bull elk, NW Wyoming.

Black Bear *(Ursus americanus)*

The predatory behavior of black bears is similar to that described for brown bears, but is relatively more "delicate." There may be more evidence of claw marks on the carcass, and black bears may be more likely than brown bears to move the carcass into thick cover without caching. Tracks are important for identifying the presence of bears. In geographical regions where black and brown bears overlap, it is important use track characteristics and hair identification to distinguish between the two species. **The Palmisciano Method is a distinguishing method when using a track from the front foot (Appendix C, Bear Family).** In addition, scat size can add information, but caution should be used due to similarities between species. Although the size/age of a bear are important, moisture content and fiber are critical factors affecting scat size (James Halfpenny, personal communication).

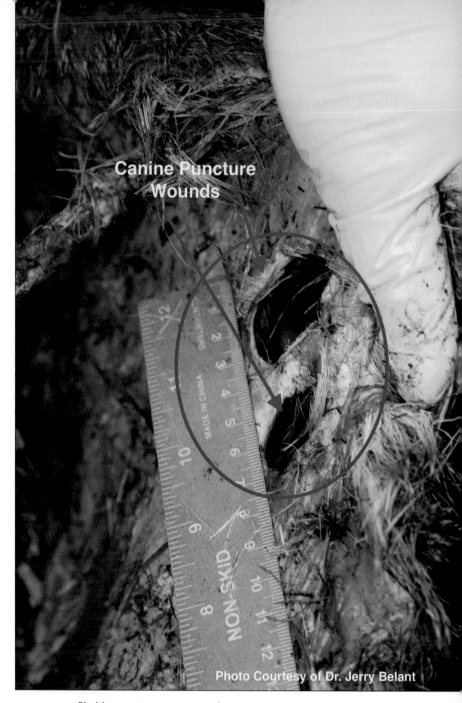

Canine Puncture Wounds

Photo Courtesy of Dr. Jerry Belant

Black bear canine puncture wounds.

Cache

Photo Courtesy of Dr. Jerry Belant

Black bear cache, white-tailed deer.

Female black bear kill, white-tailed deer.

Gray Wolf (*Canis lupus*)

Wolves pursue their prey, biting and holding on until they go down through trauma and exhaustion. **Attack points are numerous and often found from rear to front including: flanks, haunches, "armpits," lower front shoulders, throat, and muzzle.** One contributor described their attack as often starting from the rear and moving forward as the pursuit progresses. They tend to bite and hold on, causing heavy tissue damage. Many of the bites are crushing, but may not puncture the hide of larger prey. Tracks are an important piece of evidence for determining how the prey was killed and the presence of wolves at the kill site.

Massive hemorrhaging, upon skinning, is evident in the flanks, haunches, "armpits," lower front shoulders, and often the muzzle or throat. The wolf often suffocates the prey.

Torn skin and hemorrhaging on hind leg by wolves, Yellowstone National Park (YNP).

morrhaged bite tear on hind leg

Photo Courtesy of Dr. Claire Gower

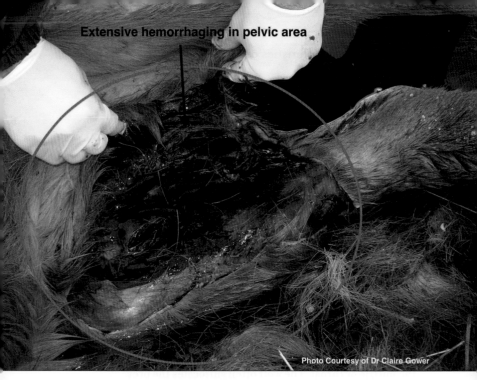

Extensive hemorrhaging in pelvic area

Photo Courtesy of Dr Claire Gower

Extensive hemorrhaging in the pelvic area of elk killed by wolves, YNP.

Hemorrhaging around bite/tear from wolves, YNP.

Hemorrhaging around bite/tear

Photo Courtesy of Dr Claire Gower

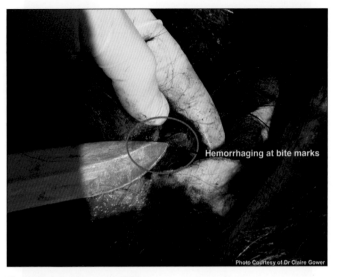

Hemorrhaging at bite mark, YNP.

Canids in general are the "messiest" eaters. Because wolves don't cache, they are competing more directly with avian and other scavengers and so move fast and eat fast. Wolves in a pack will grab and rip off parts and pieces, then move off a short distance to eat their morsels. If a pack is involved, feeding trails and bed sites may be evident in a spoke-like fashion around the carcass.

Wolves, especially in packs, will eat all parts of the body and in multiple places. The rumen and intestines get spread out; sometimes only portions are consumed. Big bones will be gnawed heavily and ribs are often chewed down to the vertebrae. An adult elk can be consumed quickly, in two to three days.

Bull elk killed and fed on by wolves, YNP.

Elk killed and fed on by wolves (note extensive chewing of ribs), YNP.

Coyote (*Canis latrans*)

Coyotes are important predators of mule deer, antelope, and white-tailed deer fawns, elk calves, and smaller adult deer and antelope (Hamlin et. al. 1984, Pac and White 2007, Christopher et. al. 2007, Barrett 1984, Ballard et. al. 1999, Ballard et. al. 2001, Barber-Meyer et. al. 2008). However, sizes of prey and environmental factors have to fit the predator. For example, it is unlikely a coyote will kill a mature buck in good condition during summer.

Like wolves, coyotes pursue their prey. On larger prey, the **pursuit can go on for a long time** and usually results in heavy trauma and exhaustion.

Attack points on larger prey are similar to wolves, but lower on the legs, below the haunches and shoulders. The nose, throat at the angle of the jaw, and back of the neck are the primary attack points on smaller prey (fawns, calves). On larger prey, the belly/udder region is also an attack point. Again, hemorrhaging will be obvious in these areas. On larger prey, hemorrhaging from coyotes is not as "deep" in muscle tissue as compared to wolves. Canine punctures are relatively small compared to wolves. Also differing from wolves, coyotes are known to exhibit caching behavior. Tracks are important in determining the presence of coyotes at the kill site, both for how the animal was killed and the differentiation between coyotes and wolves.

Antelope fawn killed by coyotes, Colorado.

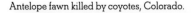

Canine puncture on antelope killed by coyotes, Colorado.

Coyote cache of antelope fawn, Colorado.

Bobcat (*Lynx rufus*)

Studies have shown that bobcats can be significant predators of mule deer, white-tailed deer, antelope, and wild sheep fawns/lambs (Rolling et. al. 1945, Ballard et. al. 1999, Barrett 1984, Beale and Smith 1973). Bobcats will also kill adult deer opportunistically (Marston 1942, Rolling 1945) and appear to attack riding on the back, biting at the neck. **Attack points are the neck just behind the head, followed by suffocation** as the ultimate cause of death. Most carcasses of young ungulates are **dragged or carried from the kill site** and often **cached with light surface debris**.

Where bobcat and Canada lynx range overlap, track size and stride length are the best distinguishing characteristics. Bobcat front foot widths are seldom wider than 2.25 inches, while lynx front foot widths are 3.75 inches or larger (Appendix C, excerpts from *A Field Guide to Mammal Tracking in North America*, Halfpenny, 1986). Bobcat tracks are also

Bobcat canine puncture wounds, white-tailed deer.

Bobcat cache, white-tailed deer.

distinguished by definitive pad prints, while lynx often leave no distinguishable pad prints because their foot is covered in dense hair. In snow, lynx tracks leave a "halo" appearance due to their densely haired feet (personal communication, Brian Giddings, retired furbearer biologist, Montana Fish, Wildlife and Parks).

Canada Lynx (*Lynx canadensis*)

Most of the studies in North America overwhelmingly find that lynx predate on small mammals, primarily snowshoe hares. However, research has shown that they can also be significant predators on caribou calves (Bergerud 1971) and have been known to kill neonates of other species. The primary **attack point is the neck** and they will tend to **move calves to shelter away from the kill site.**

Lynx can (and occasionally do) kill adult deer, caribou, and wild sheep opportunistically (Fuller 2004, Stephenson el. al. 1991, Poszig et. al. 2004). This is most likely to occur

Lynx cache of caribou neonate, Newfoundland.

Lynx cache of caribou neonate II, Newfoundland.

Lynx feeding behavior, caribou neonate, Newfoundland.

Remains of neonate from lynx predation.

in winter, when snow conditions impede travel of prey. What has been described to occur is **riding on the back and biting at the neck near the base of the skull, similar to bobcats.** Bite and claw marks can be found in those locations.

Wolverine (*Gulo gulo*)

Although wolverines in North America are commonly thought of as scavengers of larger game and predators of smaller mammals (such as marmots), predation has been documented in caribou (*Rangifer tarandus*), primarily on neonates, during studies in British Columbia and Denali National Park in Alaska (Gustine, et. al. BC; Adams, et. al. Denali). In Norway and Sweden, wolverines are predators on reindeer (*Rangifer tarandus*), roe deer (*Capreolus capreolus*), and domestic sheep (Landa, et. al. 1997, Landa et. al, 1999, Skatan et. al. 2011). Wolverines have also been documented killing larger prey on occasion, such as adult moose, but under extenuating circumstances such as the moose being mired in deep snow and unable to escape (Inman personal communication).

Caching is prevalent. Inman (2013) emphasizes that winter-kill ungulates and neonate ungulates are important food sources for wolverines. Larger prey caching is accomplished by "chunking/butchering" the animal into smaller pieces and storing the pieces in cold areas (Inman personal communication). In contrast to cougars and bears, wolverines cache in areas with existing structure, such as boulder fields, as described by Inman (2013) as "cold, structured micro-sites."

Female wolverine kill, elk neonate, head and one hind leg removed and taken to cache site one kilometer away. SW Montana.

Iverine Cache at Den Site

Photo Courtesy of Dr. Robert Inman

Wolverine cache at winter den site, SW Montana.

Based on investigations in Norway, wolverine **attack points include:** neck just behind the ears, damaging neck vertebrae, and also to head, nose, and throat (Skatan et. al. 2011).

III. Literature Cited

Adams, L. G., F. J. Singer, and B. W. Dale. 1995. Caribou calf mortality in Denali National Park, Alaska. *The Journal of Wildlife Management* 59:584-594.

Ballard, W. B., H.A. Whitlaw, S. J. Young, R. A. Jenkins, and G. J. Forbes. 1999. Predation and survival of white-tailed deer fawns in northcentral New Brunswick. *The Journal of Wildlife Management* 6:574-579.

Ballard, W. B., D. L. Lutz, T. W. Keegan, L. H. Carpenter, and J. C. deVos Jr. 2001. Deer–predator relationships: a review of recent North American studies with emphasis on mule and black-tailed deer. *Wildlife Society Bulletin* 29:99-115.

Barber-Meyer, S. M., L. D. Mech, and P. J. White. 2008. Elk calf survival and mortality following wolf restoration to Yellowstone National Park. Wildlife Monographs No. 169: pp 1-30.

Barrett, M. W. 1984. Movements, habitat use, and predation on pronghorn fawns in Alberta. *The Journal of Wildlife Management* 48:542-550.

Beale, D. M., and A. D. Smith. 1973. Mortality of pronghorn antelope fawns in western Utah. *The Journal of Wildlife Management* 37:343-352.

Bergerud, A. 1971. The population dynamics of Newfoundland caribou. Wildlife Monograph 25: pp 1–55.

Bergman, D. L., W. Sparklin, C. Carrop, J. A. Schmidt,III, S.
Bender, and S. Breck. 2010. Depredation investigation:
Using canine spread to identify the predator species.
In. Proc. 24th Vertebr. Pest Conf., R. M. Timm and K.A.
Fagerstone, Eds., Published at the Univ. of Calif., Davis.
pp 304-307.

Cheatum, E. L. 1949. Bone marrow as an index of malnutri-
tion in deer. *New York Conservationist* 3:19-22.

Christopher, N. J., J. A. Jenks, J. D. Sievers, D. E. Roddy, and
F. G. Lyndzey. 2007. Survival of pronghorns in western
South Dakota. *The Journal of Wildlife Management* 71:
737-743.

Dillon, L.C. 1997. Insect succession on carrion in three bio-
geoclimatic zones of British Columbia. Thesis, Simon
Fraser Universtiy. pp 76.

Fuller, A. K. 2004. Canada lynx predation on white-tailed
deer. *Northeastern Naturalist* 11(4):395-398.

Gonder, F. C. 2008. Wildlife decomposition in west-central
Montana: A preliminary study conducted to provide field
investigation material and training for wildlife officers.
Professional paper for Thesis, Criminology and Forensics Anthropology, University of Montana. pp 106.

Greer, K. R. 1968. A compression method indicates fat content of elk (Wapiti) femur marrow. *The Journal of Wildlife
Management* 32:747-751.

Gustine, D. D., K.L. Parker, R. J. Lau, M. P. Gillingham, and
D. C. Heard. 2006. Calf survival of woodland caribou in
a multi-predator ecosystem. Wildlife Monographs 165:
pp 1-31.

Halfpenny, J. C. 1986. A field guide to mammal tracking in North America., illustrated by E. Biesiot. Johnson Books, Boulder, CO. 161 pages.

Halfpenny, J. C., and T. D. Furman. 2010. Tracking wolves: the basics. *A Naturalist's World*, PO Box 989, Gardiner, MT. 37 pages.

Halfpenny, J. C. 2008. Scats and tracks of North America, a field guide to the signs of nearly 150 wildlife species, illustrated by T. Telander. Falcon Guides, Guilford, CT and Helena, MT. 327 pages.

Hamlin, K. L., R. S. Riley, D. B. Pyrah, A. D. Dood, and R. J. Mackie. 1984. Relationships among mule deer fawn mortality, coyote and alternate prey species. *The Journal of Wildlife Management* 48:488-499.

Husseman, J. S. 2003. Correlation patterns of marrow fat in Rocky Mountain elk bones. *The Journal of Wildlife Management* 67:742-746.

Inman, R. M. 2013. Wolverine ecology and conservation in the western United States. Dissertation, Faculty of Natural Resources and Agricultural Sciences, Department of Ecology, Uppsala, Sweden No. 2013:448 pages.

Landa, A., O. Strand, J. E. Swenson, and T Skogland. 1997. Wolverine and their prey in southern Norway. *Canadian Journal of Zoology* 15:1292-1299.

Landa, A., K. Gudvangen, J. E. Swenson, and E. Roskaft. 1999. Factors associated with wolverine *Gulo gulo* predation on domestic sheep. *Journal of Applied Ecology 36*:963-973.

Marston, M. A. 1942. Winter relationships of bobcats to white-tailed deer in Maine. *The Journal of Wildlife Management* 6:328-337.

Mech, C. D., and G. D. DelGiudice. 1985. Limitations of the marrow-fat technique as an indicator of body condition. *Wildlife Society Bulletin* 13:204-206.

Moore, T. D., L. E. Spence, C. E. Dugnolle, and W. G. Hepworth. 1995. Identification of the dorsal guard hairs of some mammals of Wyoming. Bulletin, Wyoming Game and Fish Commission, No. 14.

O'Gara, B. W. Unknown date. Differential characteristics of predator kills. Montana Cooperative Wildlife Research Unit, University of Montana, Missoula. 15 pages.

Pac, D. F., and G. C. White. 2007. Survival and cause-specific mortality of male mule deer under different hunting regulations in the Bridger Mountains, Montana. *The Journal of Wildlife Management* 77:816-827.

Payne, J. A. 1965. A summer carrion study of the baby pig *"Sus scrofa." Ecology* 46:592-602.

Poszig, D., C. D. Apps, and A. Dibb. 2004. Predation on two mule deer, *Odocoileus hemionus*, by a Canada lynx, *Lynx canadensis*, in the southern Canadian Rocky Mountains. *Canadian Field Naturalist* 118:191-194.

Quimby, D. C., and J. E. Gaab. 1957. Mandibular dentition as an age indicator in Rocky Mountain Elk. *The Journal of Wildlife Management* 21:435-451.

Roffe, T, J., and T. m. Work. 2005. Wildlife health and disease investigations. In Braun, C. E. editor, *Techniques for Wildlife Investigations and Management*, 6th edition, The Wildlife Society, Bethesda, Maryland. pp 197-212.

Rolling, C. T. 1945. Habits, foods and parasites of the bobcat in Minnesota. *The Journal of Wildlife Management* 9: 131-145.

Skatan, J. E., and M. Loventzen. 2011. Killed by predators? Manual for documentation of predator damage to livestock and domesticated reindeer. *Norweigian Nature*, Directorate for Nature Management, Tondheim, Norway 120 pages.

Stephenson, R. O., D. V. Grangaard, and J. Burch. 1991. Lynx predation on red fox, caribou, and Dall sheep in Alaska. *Canadian Field Naturalist* 105:255-262.

Stroud, DVM, R.D. Unknown date. Wildlife field forensic technique. Ashland, OR: US Fish and Wildlife Service, National Fish and Wildlife Forensics Lab.

The Palmisciano Method, Unk. Date. In westernwildlife.org, for Western Wildlife Outreach.

IV. Appendix A

A field sampling kit used by Montana Fish, Wildlife and Parks

Includes: tape measure (six-foot/three-meter), ruler, vernier caliper, waterproof pens, data cards, sterile disposable scalpels, nine milliliter serum separator blood tubes, swab with media tube, tweezers, 35 cc syringes and needles (1.5 inch, 18 gauge), latex gloves, particulate respirator/surgical mask

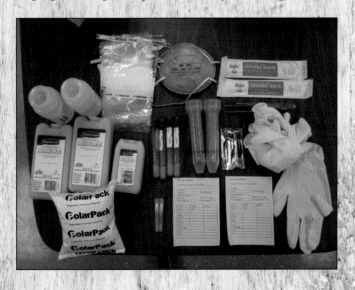

(3M N95), four-ounce and eighteen-ounce Whirl-Pak bags, two eight-ounce Nalgene bottles with four ounces of formalin, polar pack, blue ice. All of the above can be placed in a small cooler.

And, don't forget the camera!

V. Appendix B

KILL EVALUATION AND CATEGORIZATION CHART

LIST NUMBERS THAT APPLY ON PREY CARCASS FORM

Carnivore Kill:

1. Sign of Struggle evident
   a. Scuff or track evidence of chase and struggle
   b. Blood and hair on ground from pursuit
   c. Broken branches
   d. Blood on trees
2. SubQ Hemorrhage on hide/carcass
3. Aspirated blood in trachea, mouth, nose.

CARNIVORE	POSSIBLE	PROBABLE	POSITIVE
COUGAR	4. Old cougar trx. discernable by shape and stride pattern only.	9. Fresh cougar tracks discernable by detailed toe and pad arrangement.	20. Canine punctures to back of neck, or at throat.
	5. Ungulate prey hair in small "clumps" around carcass has appearance of being sheared off or cut near root base.	10. Carcass remains concealed near tree &/or brush.	21. Hemorrhage to back of neck or at throat near jawline.
		11. Carcass remains not scattered, but clustered in area < 30 m.	22. Claw marks or claw tracks apparent along neck, shoulders, or back, or face.
	6. Feces covered in "toilet" but dry or chalky in appearance.	12. Remains buried/cached w/ light debris such as plucked hair, small sticks, leaf-needle-soil duff. During winter, caches may be completely of snow packed on top of carcass.	
	7. Toilets, scrapes, bed sites not apparent or appear weathered.	13. Cougar feces dark, moist, or liquid.	23. Drag marks to cache/concealment site with ungulate prey hair along drag line.
		14. Toilets and/or scrapes appear recently created.	
		15. Tree scratching at site.	24. Kill not scavenged by bear or wolf.
	8. Carcass remains in dense cover, small drainage or side draw.	16. Two–four bed sites oriented upslope from carcass and concealed at base of tree, against boulder or rock outcrop.	25. Canine holes measure 4.5 to 5.7 cm apart for top canine punctures &/or 3.0 to 4.5 cm apart for bottom pair.
		17. Bedsites contain cougar hair.	
		18. Rumen rejected as food, possibly buried/cached.	
		19. Presence of cougar via visual, tracks, or radio-location.	

(continued)

(CONTINUED)

CARNIVORE	POSSIBLE	PROBABLE	POSITIVE
WOLF	26. Old wolf trx. discernable by shape and stride pattern only. 27. Carcass remains in open habitat with ≤ canopy cover. 28. Feces in open and not covered; feces dry or chalky in appearance; or no feces present at all.	29. Fresh wolf tracks discernable by detailed toe and pad arrangement. 30. Carcass remains scattered possibly >300 m from the kill site. 31. No bed sites evident. 32. If bed sites evident, generally more than 2–4 bed sites oriented in "spoke-wheel" fashion around kill site; bedsites in open on grass or under canopy cover, but not necessarily at base of tree. 33. Bedsites contain wolf hair. 34. Radio-collared wolves at or in vicinity of kill.	35. Hemorrhage apparent on hide at back of metatarsus and femur areas. 36. If any hide or organs left to examine on head at throat: canine punctures to throat on cows and calves. 37. No cougar or bear sign at site. 38. Canine holes measure 4.5 to 5.3 cm apart for top canine punctures &/or 3.0 to 4.0 cm apart for bottom pair.
BEAR	39. Old bear tracks discernable by shape or as depressions in soil only. 40. Carcass may be in open (generally grizzly bear) or forest cover (generally black bear).	41. Recent bear tracks that show track details. 42. Moist/wet bear scats in vicinity or on outer perimeter of bedsites. 43. Bedsites within meters of carcass or next to carcass. 44. Bedsites contain bear hair. 45. Grizzly or black bear hair on antlers, trees, or brush. 46. Carcass buried with large amount of material including large sticks and dirt; area has churned or roto-tilled appearance indicative of Grizzly bear. 47. Carcass in tree cover or draw, but not cached—more indicative of Black bear. 48. Hide on carcass is inverted over the head and down legs resulting in a "banana-peel" appearance. 49. Viscera consumed as food.	50. Bear sign only; no other cougar or wolf sign present. 51. Broken neck-rift on occipital condyle/cervical vertebrae. 52. Extensive bruising on back of hind quarters, ribs and/or shoulders. 53. Bite marks to spine behind shoulders. 54. Canine puncture holes measure 5.5 to 6.5 for upper canines & 5.5 to 6.5 for lower canines for grizzly bears and 4.5 to 5.5 for lower canines on black bears.

Note: Bears in Yellowstone scavenge carcasses (winter kill, cougar and wolf kills) during spring, so make sure no other carnivore sign is evident at the site. Bear predation in YNP is generally directed at calves and fawns where most of the carcass is entirely consumed; or bison kills (Grizzly bears).

VI. Appendix C

Includes fifteen pages from Halfpenny, 1986,
A Field Guide to Mammal Tracking in North America,
to aid the investigator in identifying predator
track and scat evidence.

Please note: People using the *Predation ID Manual* are also encouraged to acquire one or all of the following:

a. Halfpenny 1986, *A Field Guide to Mammal Tracking in North America*

b. Halfpenny 2008, *Scats and Tracks of North America*, a field guide to the signs of nearly 150 wildlife species, illustrated by T. Telander

c. Halfpenny and Furman 2010, *Tracking Wolves: The Basics*

Any of these guides will greatly enhance the individual's knowledge of track and scat identification.

SCAT PHOTOGRAPHS

Color photographs have been provided to illustrate the great variation in scats. In order to show detail, within the scat, we took close-up photographs of a portion of the cords of a scat pile or of a few pellets of a clump. Remember, when observing, that the total quantity of scat is a good relative indicator of species size within a group.

For ease of comparison, all photographs were taken against the same background and scale. The white fibers you will occasionally see stuck to the scat in the photographs are cotton packing material.

Abbreviations for sources of specimens: MC for Murie Collection, Teton Science School; 1/2c for the author's material; YNP for Yellowstone National Park; CNP for Canyonlands National Park; DNP for Denali National Park; RMNP for Rocky Mountain National Park; GSD for Great Sand Dunes National Monument; JH for Jackson Hole; ACES for Aspen Center of Environmental Sciences; TSS for Teton Science School; NR for Niwot Ridge; and MRS for the Mountain Research Station. Both NR and MRS are located west of Boulder, Colorado. The photography is by Tom Schenck, Camren, Inc.

1. **Red Fox.** The lower scat contains mostly by-products of the digestion of animal protein; the upper scat contains more hair and is lighter in color. (Sawhill ponds, Boulder, CO, 1/2c)

2. **Coyote.** The upper scat contains vegetable material; blades of grass are obvious. The lower scat contains mostly deer hair, but the darkness in the center indicates that some meat was left on the carcass. (NR, 1/2c)

3. **Wolf.** This scat is composed entirely of caribou hair, indicating that there was not much meat left on the carcass. (DNP, MC)

4. **Bobcat.** Definite segments identify this cat scat. Scat from drier regions is more segmented than that from non-desert areas. (Sheldon Range, NV, MC)

5. **Lynx.** Segmentation identifies this as cat scat, and the dark color indicates that the lynx was eating an animal protein diet. (DNP, MC)

6. **Mountain Lion.** A large portion of this scat is deer hair, but some animal protein is present. The number of bone fragments indicates that the lion ate several bones. Perhaps this scat represents the final remnants of a carcass. (Rabbit Ears Pass, CO, 1/2c)

7. **Weasel.** This scat from a small weasel is composed of hair and animal protein. (MRS, 1/2c)

8. **Mink.** The scat on the right contains numerous pieces of crayfish exoskeleton, while the one on the left contains fur, possibly that of a jumping mouse. (RMNP, 1/2c)

9. **Mink.** The scat on the right contains fish scales and animal protein; that on the left contains fur, possibly that of a muskrat. (RMNP, 1/2c)

10. **Marten.** This scat is composed of animal protein and is formed into looped cords. (MRS, 1/2c)

11. **Striped Skunk.** The scat is fairly large in diameter and must be from a large animal. The silverish color is due to varnish. The black in the lower left corner is the true color. (Elk Refuge, JH, WY, MC)

12. **River Otter.** Composed of fish scales, this scat is very fragile. Individual scales and vertebrae reflect light in the photograph. (JH, WY, 1/2c)

13. **Raccoon.** The omnivorous diet of the raccoon is shown by this coarse scat containing animal protein, bits of bones, and vegetation. (ACES, CO, 1/2c)

14. **Ringtail.** The scat on the left is mostly animal protein; the one on the right is composed of vegetable matter. (Nevada?, MC)

15. **Black Bear.** The scat is composed entirely of grass. (YNP, 1/2c)

16. **Black Bear.** The bear was feeding on a fresh elk carcass and the scat is mostly animal protein. The few pieces of vegetation in the scat may have been in the stomach or intestinal tract of the elk. (Gros Ventre Mtns., WY, 1/2c)

17. **Black Bear.** Seeds of pin cherry and snowberry are present in this fragile and easily broken scat. (MRS, 1/2c)

18. **Black Bear.** The woody fragments are acorn shells. (Sangre De Cristo mountains near GSD, 1/2c)

19. **Grizzly Bear.** The woody fragments are pine nuts. (YNP, MC)

20. **Grizzly Bear.** Diameter is about 2½ in (6.4 cm). (YNP, MC)

21. **Grizzly Bear.** The slight blue tint in this scat indicates a diet of blueberries. Blueberry leaves are also visible. (Glacier National Park, 1/2c)

22. **Pika.** Round pellets characterize the rabbit order. (NR, 1/2c)

23. **Cottontail Rabbit.** The faint green color indicates moist vegetation; plant fragments are visible. (CNP, 1/2c)

24. **Cottontail Rablbit.** After the early snows, cottontails were feeding on lodgepole pine twigs. Scat and twig tips were present under low hanging branches. (MRS, 1/2c)

25. **Snowshow Hare.** The black pellets on the left are the nutrient-rich pellets that rabbits re-ingest. The other pellets are the ones usually found. (MRS, 1/2c)

26. **Jackrabbit.** Scat from the whitetailed jackrabbit were obtained near Rand, CO. (1/2c)

27. **Beaver.** These scats are composed mostly of coarse woody chips. (Snake River, JH, WY, MC)

28. **Chickaree (Pine Squirrel).** The soft, amorphous pellets indicate a moist diet. (MRS, 1/2c)

29. **Golden-mantled Ground Squirrel.** Soft, amorphous squirrel pellets indicate a moist diet. (MRS, l/2c)

30. **Chickaree.** Additional signs, including pine cone scales and pieces of twigs, were found with this scat. The whiter pellets have been attacked by fungus. The three dark pellets in center are the natural color. (MRS, 1/2c)

31. **Marmot.** Marmots usually produce dark amorphous pellets that are much larger than those of the rest of the squirrels. These may look like marten scats, but the presence of many scats at a latrine indicates marmots. (NR, 1/2c)

32. **Porcupine.** Porcupines produce red-colored pellets during the winter when they are feeding mostly on conifers. (Mt. Evans, CO, 1/2c)

33. **Porcupine.** Porcupines produce black or dark pellets during the summer when they feed mostly on grasses, herbs, and shrubs. (MRS, 1/2c)

34. **Pocket Gopher.** Woody material and grass blades are present in these gopher scats. (*Thomomys talpoides,* NR, 1/2c)

35. **Mule Deer.** The nipple-dimple shape, more often associated with elk pellets, is apparent. (Teton National Forest, 1/2c) See also antelope scat.

36. **Mule Deer.** These small pellets came from a known-age, 18-month old deer. They are smaller than those of an adult deer. (ACES, CO, 1/2c)

37. **Mule Deer.** These pellets were very soft because of a moist spring diet. After they were deposited, they dried and bleached to a light brown. (CNP, 1/2c)

38. **Mule Deer.** The deer that produced these pellets was eating on a dry woody diet. The pellets, although small, resemble moose pellets. (CNP, 1/2c)

39. **Elk.** The nipple-dimple shape is apparent on these pellets, but the nipple end is rounded. The scat were produced on August 22, 1979 when the vegetation had started to dry out. (NR, 1/2c)

40. **Elk.** A moist diet in the spring formed soft pellets that stuck together in this large clump. (NR, 1/2c)

41. **Elk.** Large elk scat produced in July on a moist diet. (YNP, 1/2c)

42. **Moose.** These pellets were from a yearling moose browsing on woody vegetation. In color and shape, they are the same as those produced by adults, but they are smaller. (YNP, 1/2c)

43. **Moose.** Pellets produced from a moist diet of stream vegetation in October. (TSS, WY, 1/2c)

44. **Antelope.** These scats, produced in the winter, are longer than usual. I have also noticed the tendency for mule deer scats produced during winter to be longer than those produced the rest of the year. (Near Walden, CO, 1/2c)

45. **Big Horn Sheep.** A dry early June diet produced these separate pellets. (Mt. Evans, CO, 1/2c)

46. **Buffalo.** A calf, grazing on dry feed, produced this hard, layered scat. Its small size is due to the small size of the calf. (YNP, 1/2c)

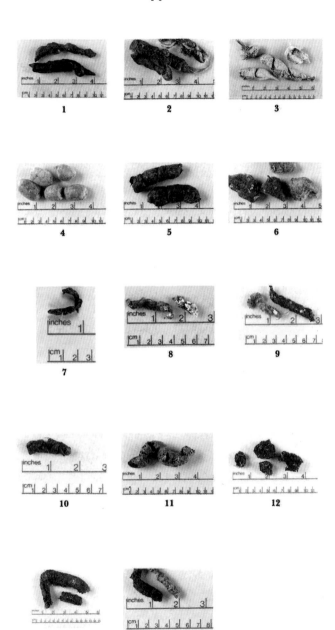

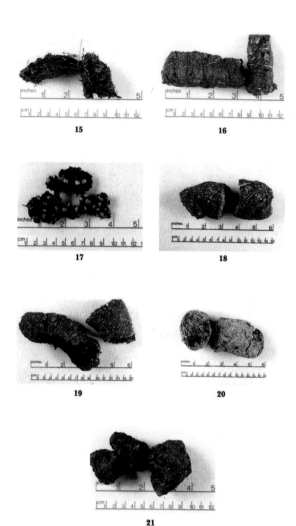

15

16

17

18

19

20

21

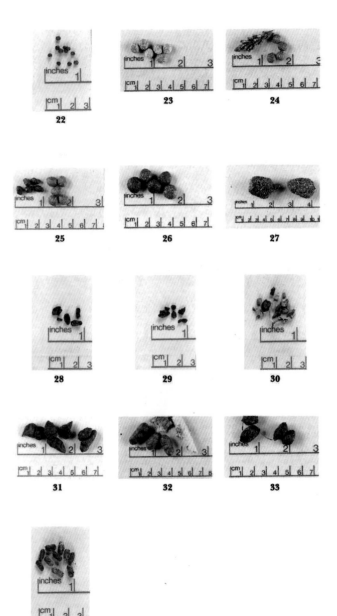

15

16

17

18

19

20

21

Contents

Some materials we find in the scat may help us identify the mammals that left them. Fish scales suggest mink or otter. Crayfish parts may indicate mink or otter, but more likely the predator was a raccoon. Berries and nuts are indicative of bears. Regrettably, aluminum foil and plastic are found in scat; they tell us the mammals have been feeding on garbage.

Odor

Scat containing a large amount of animal protein has a rather strong disagreeable odor, whereas carnivore scat containing grass or especially berries may be very sweet smelling. Mustelid scat, when fresh, has a characteristic musky odor that most people can recognize. Many people believe that they can recognize the odor of fresh fox scat.

Position

Naturalist, writer, and artist Ernest Thompson Seton recognized the importance of the method and location of scat disposal in relation to the social structure and home maintained by mammals. Animals that defecate many times per day (deer defecate 20 or more times per day) cannot have one den site but must move around. Mammals that maintain one home have evolved a method of **sanitation**, including scat disposal. These mammals have longer intestines that absorb more material, allowing them to defecate only once or twice per day. Three systems of scat disposal were recognized by Seton: the **wet system**, including the use of streams; the **dry system**, including isolation and burial; and the **parasitic** or **antiseptic system**, including insect and fungal decomposition. Scat disposal may also reflect a mammal's methods of communication. The location and position of scat deposition therefore relates directly to the lifestyle of mammals.

When prominently displayed, scat deposits may serve as a **territorial marking.** For instance, I have observed bears depositing scat on the scat of other animals, including domestic cows. Many different mammals may deposit scat and urine regularily at a **sign post.** These places must serve some purpose in communication that we humans cannot fully appreciate. Residents and visitors alike leave their calling cards at these sign posts. They serve as a record of who lives in the area and who has passed through.

Dogs may use forks in the trail, old carcasses, or prominent knobs as sign posts. Cats tend to bury their scat. **Burial** is more common on the hunting trail and less common near the den where the presence of scat may be serving as a territorial marking. Cats and dogs will also use mounds formed by ants as defecation points. River otters use downed logs, rocks, or prominent protrusions on the bank. Otters not only leave scat at these points but also mark with anal scent glands. The marking appears to be associated with tufts of grass. Bears, when feeding for several days on one carcass, will leave many scats around their day beds.

Rodents may use prominent scent posts that are natural in origin, constructed, or of human origin. Beavers and muskrats make **scent posts** of mud and matted grasses where they mark with anal glands. Once in a while you may find scat at these scent posts. Usually, you will find muskrat scat on logs in the water just above the water level. Beavers usually deposit their scat in the water. Other rodents tend to deposit scat on open patches of soil or bare objects such as cardboard or wood. You can use this tendency to take a census of the rodents in an area. Lay pieces of **tile** or cardboard in a grid on the ground and check them daily. By using food (grains) color-coded with **dyes,** you can delineate home ranges by mapping where colored scat occur on the tiles.

Many rodents have **latrines** where they defecate regularly. Some examples include voles, pocket gophers, kangaroo rats, and packrats. Gophers and kangaroo rats have underground rooms in their tunnels which are reserved for latrines. In the drier country of the southwest, packrat **middens** (dens) may be coated with scat and urine deposits dating back thousands of years. These deposits also include vegetation from the time of deposition. Analyses of the vegetation provides us detailed information about the climate when the scat were deposited. A section through the deposit reveals climatic change over the centuries.

Many animals use water to dispose of scat. Bobcats living near streams will deposit their scat in the water. This is also true for beavers and occasionally for raccoon.

Ungulates, especially moose and elk, tend to defecate in or very near their **day beds** immediately after rising. You may see large deposits of scat from sheep on the prominent ridges where they congregate. While grazing, ungulates are on the move, and pellets tend to be spread out in grassy areas.

Habitat

It is worth repeating the importance of the stage-setting clue—habitat—in limiting the possible identification of scat.

Photographs

We have provided four pages of color photographs to illustrate the rich details found in scat. As you read the following discussion of scat refer often to the color plates. See pages 73–76.

SCAT COMPARISONS

Dog Family

Dog family scats are thick cords and occasionally folded cords. The end of the scat that leaves the anus last has a pointed tail. When the scats are broken into several parts, only the last segment has a tail. Colors which are diet dependent include white, gray, brown, and black. Often large items are present in the scat. These include seeds, insect remains, grass, feathers, hair, teeth, and small bones. Insect remains often include beetle elytra (hardened forewings) and grasshopper legs. Pieces of vegetation may constitute small portions of each scat. These parts were probably in the stomachs of herbivores when they were eaten. When canines feed on vegetation, the whole scat is usually composed of plant material. Dogs ingest small rocks while feeding on other items.

You will detect an acrid odor associated with fresh canine scat. Many naturalists feel that the odor is stronger during the mating season. Dogs use scat and urine for territorial markings and deposit them in elevated positions. You may find scratch marks near the scat. These scratchings, which are made by the hind feet, probably help to circulate the associated odors (see Plate 6). Often several scats will be deposited at the same point over the course of several days.

Cat Family

Cat scats are broken cords with relatively short tails, or they may be semisoft. Colors include brown, white, gray, and black depending on the proportions of prey items. Portions of prey items including insect chitin (outer shell), feathers, hair, bones, and teeth may be found in scat. Berries may be prominent in the fall, and other plants may occasionally compose the main portion of the scat.

Cat scat and urine have a strong odor and are used for territorial marking. Scat is deposited on elevated points (tree stumps and rocks) near the edges of the home range and on hunting trails. Near dens, both scat and urine are deposited in shallow holes and then covered (see Plate 7). Scratch markings around the scat are made with the front feet.

Weasel Family

Weasel family scats are folded cords with long tails often at both ends. Colors include black and brown with occasional gray. A distinct mustelid odor is associated with fresh scat. The hard scat of weasels, martens, ferrets, minks, and wolverines are similar in appearance and differ mainly in size and habitat. These scats are relatively long, folded cords and are generally dark gray or black as the diet of these animals is mostly protein. Splinters of bones, hair, and feathers are often found in the scat. Mink scat may contain fish scales or parts of crayfish. If the mink has been feeding on frogs or fish, the scat may vary from soft to semi-liquid. Minks deposit scat on elevated objects such as logs or rocks. Ferret scat is mostly deposited below ground.

Fresh otter scat is black and slimy with an oily, fish-like smell. As the scat ages, it tends to disintegrate. When otters have been feeding on fish, their scat is very fragile and disintegrates easily. Scat may be deposited at sign posts or singly along the bank.

Badger scat can be confused with coyote scat. Badgers usually deposit their scat below ground. Some dens, when excavated, have contained short tunnels with many scats, while other dens did not contain any at all.

Droppings from skunks tend to have blunter ends than those from other weasels. You may find insects in the scat. Even in the winter, insects may be present in the scats because skunks dig out hibernating insects. Skunks tend to use any crack or crevice for a den, and you may find scat associated with these. Skunks also leave their scat in trails. The striped skunks make latrines.

Raccoon Family

Raccoon scats are short, thick even-diameter cords, usually with flat ends. Raccoons tend to deposit in large piles of several individual scats. Color is black to brown, reddish, or even bleached white. The scat has a characteristic granular appearance. You will see particles of food in raccoon scat. As raccoons are omnivorous, many different items may be found in their scat. The presence of fish and crayfish will help you differentiate their scat from that of other carnivores. Scat will be deposited on branches or limbs, and latrines are often used repeatedly. Single raccoon scats not in piles can be confused with that of other carnivores, so look for other clues when you suspect raccoons.

Scats of the ringtail are variable, depending on the diet of this omnivorous mammal. Scats are cords, often with tapered ends. Sometimes the end will be flat. Color is brown to bleached white. Scats are relatively long. Those composed of vegetable parts tend to break up.

I have observed coati scat only in the Murie Collection at the Teton Science School. The scats were thick cords with flat ends. Their color was brown. In general, they resembled those of raccoons and are probably quite variable, again depending on the omnivorous diet.

Bear Family

Bear scats are thick cords with blunt ends. The quantity of scat is often great, and you may see large piles. The omnivorous bears have brown, black, and blue-colored scat from eating pine nuts, animal protein, and berries respectively. Bear scat often contains insects, especially ants, termites, and bees. You may have to look hard at the scat to identify the undigested heads of these insects. Plant remains are also common, with grasses, dandelions, horsetails, and thistles being favored. Some scat containing plant material will be black. The fibrous nature of the scat and sweeter plant smell will separate these scat from those containing animal protein. In the fall, a diet of acorns produces above-average-size brown scat. From April to October, grizzlies will raid the caches of squirrels for white-bark pine nuts, and the remains will be evident in the scat. A fall diet of berries will produce soft to semi-liquid scat.

Scats greater than 2 inches (5 cm) in diameter have been considered grizzly scat. However, Herrero reported that of 140 grizzly scats measured in Banff National Park, 60 (58%) were less than 2 inches. Larger grizzlies produce larger scat. If you use the two-inch rule, you will tend to misidentify the females, who may be with their young, and young males, a very serious error.

Lagomorphs

Lagomorphs form two types of scat: the semi-soft black scat that is rich in vitamins and the normal hard scat.

Rabbit family. The hard scats of rabbits, jackrabbits, and hares are slightly flattened spheres. In softer, moist scat, one end may have a small point. Scats are deposited in small piles or just a few pellets at a time. Their color ranges from brown to brownish-green to pale green. Brown scat is produced during the winter when the diet consists mostly of browse. The greenish-colored scat reflects increased amounts of herbs and moist vegetation that is actively growing. If you break the brown pellets in two you may discover small bits of wood. Sniff them. They have a relatively sweet smell. Rabbits deposit scat at the bases of the branches on which they are browsing. They defecate before retiring, and you may find scat with the rabbit's resting **form,** a shallow depression in the ground.

Pika family. While you may find the soft vitamin-rich scat of rabbits, you will seldom observe that produced by pikas. Hard pika scats are more spherical than those produced by the rest of the lagomorphs. The scats are brown but often associated with or covered by white, nitrogenous urine deposits. Scat is deposited at latrines or on the top of the urine-coated rocks. Pika deposition areas may be identified by the presence of bright orange, nitrogen-loving lichens. Pika latrines may be associated with the boundaries of their territories and also with their food caches, which are found near the centers of the territories.

Rodents

Rodent scats are sausage-shaped. One end may have a slight point. You will see considerable variation even in the scat from one animal. Colors include reddish-brown, yellowish-brown, brown, and black. Contents are mostly plants. You will need a microscope to ascertain the diet from the finely-chewed materials. Many rodents use latrines and will defecate on smooth surfaces such as a board.

Mouse family. Mice usually defecate in a random manner but will occasionally have latrines for repeated use. Voles usually have latrines associated with their nests. Latrines constructed by voles differ from those of mice in that piles of vole scat will form a solid mass. Voles urinate on their scat, and their highly nitrogenous urine dries and forms bonds within the scat piles. The urine on the scat will be white. Packrats (also called woodrats) also have a highly nitrogenous urine that unites with scat and preserves it. Packrat scat is relatively large. Large, black, tarry masses you may see associated with woodrat dens apparently are accumulations of the black soft type of scat.

Muskrats defecate on stream banks and on logs only slightly above water level. Their scat is dark to black and often semi-liquid. In the spring the scats are prominately displayed to delineate territories. Later in the year defecation occurs primarily in the water.

Beaver family. Beavers defecate in the water. Beaver scats can be quite large, up to an inch (2.5 cm) in diameter. The scats are composed of large chunks of wood which may be apparent on the surface. These will quickly disintegrate in the water. Scat may occasionally be found floating on the water surface.

Squirrel family. Squirrels defecate on logs and stumps. Scat may be found at their main eating places associated with **middens** (refuge heaps of conifer cone scales). Individual pellets are often irregular and some may approach spherical shapes. Squirrel pellets from a single defecation will form small clumps when the diet is moist. Winter scat are darker, almost black. During the summer, insects are found in squirrel scat.

Prairie dog scats are relatively large and vary greatly from spheres to long sausages. One end tends to taper to a short tail. Colors vary from light brown to black. The brown scat contains a larger amount of woody material. Prairie dogs deposit their scat singly or in small numbers near the entrance to their burrows. Above ground latrines don't exist. I suspect that many scats are deposited below ground, perhaps in latrine rooms.

Ground squirrel scats tend to be joined by tails. A few scat will be found around the entrances to the burrows. Perhaps other scat are deposited below ground. Chipmunks deposit their scat at random.

Marmot scats exhibit great variability, ranging from sausage-shaped pellets to folded cords. The color is usually black. Deposition is at latrine sites near their burrow entrances or observation rocks. Large quantities of scat is present in these latrines.

Porcupine family. Porcupine scats are woody and tails occur frequently. Tails may join two or more scats into strings. Yellow and red scats are produced during the winter when the diet consists of greater than 70% conifers. The larger the amount of conifers, the redder the color. Black pellets are produced when porcupines feed mostly on the ground during the summer. The pellets consist of grasses, herbs, and shrubs. You may find large quantities of scat at the base of trees that porcupines have used for several days or at dens they have used in the winter.

Pocket gopher family. Gopher scats look like blunt-ended sausages. Color is usually brown. You probably won't find them during the summer since defecation occurs below ground. In the spring when snow melt reveals winter nests, you may find scats in large quantities. The scat will be scattered through the nests and the plant material packed into snow passages.

Pocket mouse family. The scat of pocket mice and kangaroo rats varies from dark green to black. It is deposited in burrows underground. Little information has been recorded about the scat of this interesting rodent family.

Ungulates

Variability in shape and color often makes it impossible for us to identify scat to the species that dropped it. The shape of ungulate scat varies considerably with moisture content; dry diets produce separate pellets, and moist diets produce semi-liquid clumps that resemble "cow-pies." Increasing moisture in the diet causes the pellets of a clump to coalesce. Pellets from drier diets exhibit a relatively large sausage shape. There is a tendency for the scat to resemble candy kisses in shape. Earlier I described the nipple-dimple pellet shape; the best example is elk scat.

Ungulates deposit pellets in large clumps or groups. Color varies from brown for drier and coarser plant material to black for moist herbaceous material. You will notice a definite ungulate odor associated with the scat and urine; it is particularly prominent during the rutting season in the fall. Often relative size is the best distinguishing factor among species.

Deer family. Deer pellets are highly variable, but drier ones tend to be blunt on one end and have a small point at the other end. Pellets may be 3/4-inch (2 cm) long. Occasionally, striations may run the length of each pellet. Elk pellets show a depression or dimple at one end and a nipple at the other end. Summer elk pellets are dark but tend to become more brown as they age. Moose pellets are rounded at both ends. I believe that the rounding at both ends of pellets is the result of a very dry, coarse, woody diet. In Canyonlands, I have collected deer pellets that were rounded at both ends and merely a miniature version of moose pellets found in Yellowstone. Elk feeding on a dry woody diet also produce pellets rounded at both ends. The outside of the deer, elk, and moose pellets does not show the composition of the diet. However, if you break the pellets open, you will see plant formation.

Pronghorn antelope family. Pellets tend to be teardrop-shaped, with one end blunt and the other pointed. The sides of pronghorn pellets are less parallel than those of the deer family. Many pellet groups have elongated pellets, which have a definite point at one end. As moisture content increases, pellets coalesce into large clumps. Often when these clumps hit the ground, they will flatten on one side. Pronghorn pellets may be hard to tell from sheep pellets where the two species occur together. I have noticed that there is a greater tendency for antelope scat to become covered with white fungus than for that of the other ungulates.

Bison and sheep family. For a large part of the year, bison or buffalo tend to leave large, up to a foot long (30 cm), semisoft patties known as **chips**. On dry feed, bison produce a layered scat with each layer stacked directly on top of the previous one. Young bison seem to leave the layered scat more than adults do. The small scat of younger bison is confusing; it is smaller than you would expect for scat coming from so large a mammal. Color is generally brown. The large scats of bison burn well when they are dried. Pioneers on the great plains used "**buffalo chips**" as their sole source of fuel for fires.

In Greenland, I found muskox scat to be of the dry pellet type. The moist, cow-pie type was not common. This may be because muskoxen must feed on dry low tundra vegetation. Muskoxen feeding on lush grass will probably produce more semi-soft scat. The color is brown.

Sheep scat shows great variability and can be very hard to tell from antelope scat where the two mammals occur together. Drier pellets tend to be elongated and rounded at both ends, although many will have a point at one end. Dry sheep pellets have a greater tendency to approach a spherical shape than do antelope pellets. In moister scat, pellets may be concave on one side and you will find clumps consisting of a few pellets. Individual pellets are hard to distinguish. Color varies from brown to black.

Mountain goat scat may be confused with sheep and deer scat, but individual pellets tend to be smaller. In the moist type, I believe that pellets may show a greater tendency towards layering. Color is brown to black.

BEAR FAMILY
f5(4) H5(4) co

Members	Front				Hind				Walking	
	Length		Width		Length		Width		Straddle	
	in	(cm)	in	(cm)	in	(cm)	in	(cm)	in	(cm)
Black bear	4½	(11)	4	(10)	7	(18)	3½	(8.9)	14	(36)
Grizzly	5½	(14)	5	(13)	10	(25)	6	(15)	20	(51)
Polar bear	5¾	(15)	9	(23)	12	(31)	9	(23)	??	??

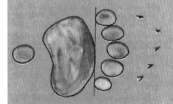

Two gait patterns
- Walking patterns
- Slow lope pattern

In a grizzly print, a line drawn from the big toe across the top of the intermediate pad intersects the little toe below the middle or may not intersect at all (after Palmisciano).

Black Bear

In a black bear print, a line drawn from the big toe across the top of the intermediate pad intersects the little toe at or above the middle (after Palmisciano).

- Hind print is human like
- Little toe may not show
- Claws don't always show
- Metacarpal pad on front foot
- Common gait is a walk

CAT FAMILY

F4 h4

Members	Front Foot				Walking			
	Length		Width		Stride		Straddle	
	in	(cm)	in	(cm)	in	(cm)	in	(cm)
Bobcat	2–	(5–)	2	(5)	22	(56)	5	(12.7)
Lynx	3¾	(10)	3¾+	(10)	28	(72)	7	(17.8)
Lion	3½	(9)	3½+	(9)	40	(102)	8	(20.3)

A plus or minus indicates that the track averages slightly larger (+) or smaller (–) than the measurement.

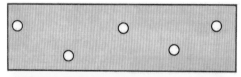

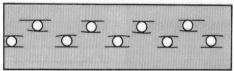

Walking gaits of lion (top) and lynx showing the greater stride of the lion.

Bobcat Front Foot   Lynx Front Foot   Lion Front Foot

- Claws generally don't show
- Prints are round or wide
- Two lobes on front of pad
- Common gait is a walk

DOG FAMILY

F4 h4 C

Members	Front Foot				Walking			
	Length		Width		Stride		Straddle	
	in	(cm)	in	(cm)	in	(cm)	in	(cm)
Kit fox	1¾	(4.4)	1½	(3.8)	14	(36)	3 –	(7.5)
Gray fox	1⅞	(4.8)	1½	(3.8)	20	(51)	3¾	(9)
Red fox	2¼	(5.7)	2	(5.0)	25	(64)	4¼	(10.7)
Arctic fox	2¼	(5.7)	2⅛	(5.4)	30	(76)	4¼	(10.8)
Coyote	2½	(6.4)	2¼	(5.7)	30	(76)	5	(12.7)
Wolf	4¾	(12.1)	4	(10.2)	40	(102)	7 +	(17.7)

A plus or minus indicates that the track averages slightly larger (+) or smaller (−) than the measurement.

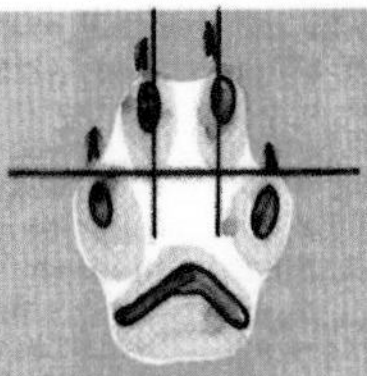

Red Fox Front Print.

- Claws generally show
- Prints longer than wide
- One lobe on front of pad
- Rotatory gallop is most common
- Compare robustness among members

■ Outer toes bigger on coyote

Lines have been added to add in judging robustness and splaying.

Coyote Front Print.

Dog Front Print.

Wolf Front Print.

WEASEL FAMILY

f5(4) H5(4) co

Members	Front Length in	(cm)	Front Width in	(cm)	Hind Length in	(cm)	Hind Width in	(cm)	Bounding Straddle in	(cm)
Weasels										
Least	⅜	(1)	½ −	(1.3)	⅜	(1)	½ −	(1.3)	1½	(3.8)
Short-tailed	½	(1.3)	½ +	(1.3)	½	(1.3)	½	(1.3)	2	(5)
Long-tailed	¾	(1.9)	¾ +	(1.9)	¾	(1.9)	¾ +	(1.9)	2½	(6.4)
Marten	1¾	(4.4)	1¾ +	(4.4)	1¾	(4.4)	1¾ +	(4.4)	3½	(23)
Fisher	2½	(6.4)	2½ +	(6.4)	2½	(6.4)	2½ +	(6.4)	6	(15)
Wolverine	4	(10)	4 +	(10)	4	(10)	4 +	(10)	9	(23)
Ferret	1⅛	(2.9)	1¼	(3.2)	1⅛	(2.9)	1¼	(3.2)	2½	(6.4)
Badger	2½	(6.4)	2 +	(5.1)	2	(5.1)	2	(5.1)	10	(25)
Mink	1¾	(4.4)	1¾ +	(4.4)	1¾	(4.4)	1¾ +	(4.4)	2¾	(7)
Otter	3¾	(9.5)	3¾ +	(9.5)	3¾	(9.5)	3¾ +	(9.5)	9	(23)
Spotted skunk	¾	(2)	1	(2.5)	1¼	(3.2)	1 −	(2.3)	2¾	(7)
Striped skunk	1½	(3.8)	1¼	(3.2)	1⅞	(4.8)	1¼	(3.2)	3½	(9)

A plus or minus indicates that the track averages slightly larger (+) or smaller (−) than the measurement.

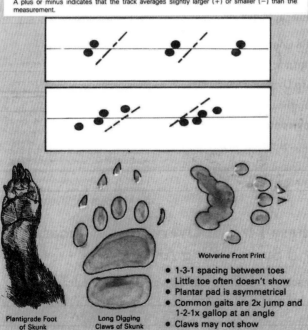

Plantigrade Foot of Skunk

Long Digging Claws of Skunk

Wolverine Front Print

- 1-3-1 spacing between toes
- Little toe often doesn't show
- Plantar pad is asymmetrical
- Common gaits are 2x jump and 1-2-1x gallop at an angle
- Claws may not show

VII. Appendix D

Predation ID Manual Data Sheet

Investigator(s) _____

Date Investigated (mm/dd/yy) _____

General Location _____

GPS Coordinates (in Decimal Degrees)

Latitude _____

Map Datum _____

Longitude _____

Environmental Factors (moisture, snow depth
and condition etc.):

_____

_____

Phase 1 Initial Overview of Carcass Site and Surrounding Area

Describe habitat, topography, aspect, terrain features:

_____

_____

_____

_____

Record observations within 200 meter radius from carcass

Note any and all sign in the larger area

Initial track identifications (see manual Appendix C, and refer to Halfpenny 1986, 2008, 2010) by family/species:

_____

_____

Check all that apply:

Evidence of Attack: ambush _____, pursuit _____, unknown _____.

Fresh: trails _____, drag trails _____, blood _____, broken twigs _____, other _____

Is there an obvious cause of death, explain:

_____

_____

_____

Phase 1 Photo ID#s /reference points _____

Phase 2 Focus on the Carcass and Immediate Carcass Site

Time of death, estimate:

_____

Condition at time of death:

   Species: _____

   Age estimate: (neonate, YOY, tooth replacement/wear): __

   _____

   Incisor collected Y/N, if Y, ID# _____

   Signs of prior injury Y/N: If Y, describe: _____

Bone marrow: healthy (white/solid/waxy) _____

malnourished (red, yet solid) _____

poor (red and gelatinous) _____

Natural death, not predation, minimal scavenging:

Explain clear absence of predation (see manual): _____

_____

_____

_____

_____

_____

Is there evidence of avian predation Y/N: domestic dog predation Y/N: if Y, explain: _____

_____

Human caused death Y/N: if Y, explain: _____

_____

Predator hair collected Y/N: if Y, ID# _____

species _____

Predator scat measurements Y/N: Scat diameter (cm)

_____,length (cm) _____, species _____

(Manual Appendix C, and refer to
Halfpenny 1986, 2008, 2010)

Predator scat collected Y/N, if Y, ID# _____

Predator track identification (Manual Appendix C, refer to
Halfpenny 1986, 2008, 2010)
Track size: FRONT (L, cm) _____ (W, cm) _____
HIND (L, cm) _____ (W, cm) _____

If walking, stride measurement (cm): _____ (use other mortality notes at end of data sheet to describe additional measurements if evidence for more than one species is found)

Felid, Ursid, Canid Evidence (Manual Table 1.)

Carcass moved/dragged to cover or cached <u>Y/N</u>
Cache w/light surface debris/hair <u>Y/N</u>
Cache w/excavation and large debris <u>Y/N</u>
Banana Peel effect on hide <u>Y/N</u>
Plucked hair <u>Y/N</u>
Inside of hide licked clean <u>Y/N/Unknown</u>
Rumen/intestine consumed <u>Y/N</u>
Latrine <u>Y/N</u>
Claw marks <u>Y/N</u>

Attack points:

Neck/throat/shoulders _____; Head/dorsal
midline (spine)/crushed vertebrae/broken pelvis _____;
 Many different attack points, legs/hindquarters/flank/
"armpits"/lower shoulders/nose _____;
Unknown _____

Initial feeding pattern:

Through rib cage/behind shoulder/lower abdomen just
anterior to pelvic juncture _____; Abdomen/other areas
_____; Abdomen/hindquarters/seemingly everywhere,
no definitive pattern _____; Unknown _____

Sign of pursuit:
None _____, Short _____, Long _____,
Unknown _____

Bed sites:

Up to 200 meters from cache/base of tree or rocks _____,
Near/on top of cache _____, Many bed sites/feeding sites
in vicinity of carcass _____, Unknown _____

Remains:

In defined area _____, Strewn all over _____,
Unknown _____

SUMMARY (check all that apply) Ursid _____,
Canid _____, Felid _____

Phase 2 photo ID#s/reference points _____

Phase 3 Investigating Carcass for Hemorrhaging (Direct evidence of predation)

Did investigator skin carcass to determine subcutaneous
hemorrhaging? Y/N
Describe sites where hemorrhaging was found: _____

_____

_____

Other direct evidence (e.g. signs of pursuit, aspirated blood,
predation observed), describe: _____

_____

_____

Canine measurement (center of hole to center of hole, cm):

_____

Phase 3 photo ID#s/reference points _____

_____

Phase 4 General Hierarchy of Scavengers and Predatory Behavior

List species of large predators present in geographic area:

_____

List, based on evidence at kill site and carcass, predator species present: _____

Is there evidence of scavenging dominance/displacement Y/N; If Y, describe: _____

_____

_____

_____

_____

Phase 5 Weight of Evidence and Event Classification

LIKELIHOOD OF PREDATION (choose one)

Definitive _____ (direct evidence, e.g. hemorrhaging, sign of pursuit/struggle, aspirated blood)

Probable _____ (Indirect evidence—multiple lines of evidence i.e. moving carcass, caching, "banana peel," rumen present, skeletal bites, bed sites, fresh track, only 1 predator present, etc.—describe evidence for each species present at the kill/carcass site for each species)

Possible _____ (scavenging dominance—describe evidence for each species present at kill/carcass site)

Unknown _____ (no direct or indirect evidence of predation, all sign old)

Not Predation _____ (little to no scavenging, signs of death other then predation)

PREDATOR IDENTIFIED based on all evidence including attack and feeding behavior ascribed to the species (Manual, Figure 2 and Part IV), and qualified based on above likelihood Classification: _____

Additional Notes: _____

_____

_____

_____

Phase 1

_____

_____

_____

Phase 2

_____

_____

_____

Additional scat measurements

_____

_____

_____

Additional track measurements

_____

_____

_____

Phase 3

_____

_____

_____

Phase 4

_____

_____

_____

_____

Phase 5

_____

_____

_____

_____